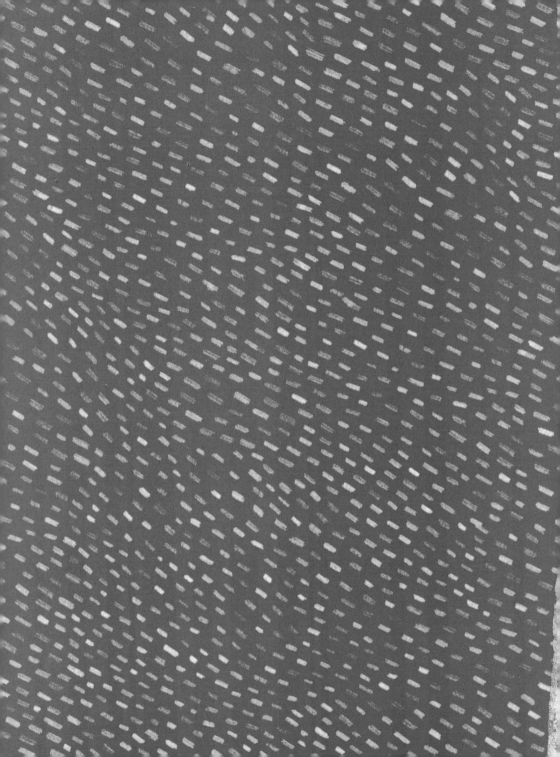

HOW TO BE A GOOD CREATURE

HOW TO
BE A GOOD
CREATURE

A MEMOIR IN THIRTEEN ANIMALS

By Sy Montgomery

Illustrated by Rebecca Green

HOUGHTON MIFFLIN HARCOURT
BOSTON · NEW YORK

Always and forever, for Dr. Millmoss

hmhco.com

The text was set in Garamond Pro.
Book design by Cara Llewellyn

The Library of Congress Cataloging-on-Publication data is on file.

ISBN: 978-0-544-93832-8 hardcover
ISBN: 978-1-328-62903-6 special markets

Printed in the United States of America
DOH 10 9 8 7 6 5 4 3 2
4500744226

All photos courtesy of the author except for: Jacqueline Anderson, 185 (top); Nic Bishop, 180
(top), 182 (top); Nic Bishop, with permission of CCF, 183; Ben Kilham, 187 (bottom); Phebe
Lewan, 187 (top); Christine MacDonald, 178 (bottom); Howard Mansfield, 181 (bottom), 188
(top); Pincus Mansfield, 188 (bottom left); Sam Marshall, 188 (bottom right); Evelyn Naglie,
189; Kate O'Sullivan, 186 (top left); Jody Simpson, 181 (top), 185 (bottom); Tianne Strombeck,
179 (bottom), 184; Barb Sylvestre, 182 (bottom); Stephanie Thomas, 186 (top right).

✳ INTRODUCTION ✳

I TRAVEL AROUND THE WORLD TO RESEARCH MY BOOKS. I joined a team of researchers radio-collaring tree kangaroos in the cloud forest of Papua New Guinea; searched for signs of snow leopards in the Altai Mountains of Mongolia's Gobi; swam with piranhas and electric eels for a book about pink dolphins in the Amazon. During all of these trips, I've thought of a saying that to me has served as a promise: When the student is ready, the teacher will appear. Though I've been blessed with some splendid classroom teachers—Mr. Clarkson, my high school journalism teacher, foremost among them—most of my teachers have been animals.

What have animals taught me about life? *How to be a good creature.*

All the animals I've known—from the first bug I must have spied as an infant, to the moon bears I met in Southeast Asia, to the spotted hyenas I got to know in Kenya—have been good creatures. Each individual is a marvel and perfect in his or her own way. Just being with any animal is edifying, for each has a knowing that surpasses human understanding. A spider can taste the world with her feet. Birds can see colors we can't begin to describe. A cricket can sing with his legs and listen with his knees. A dog can hear sounds above the level of human hearing, and can tell if you're upset even before you're aware of it yourself.

Knowing someone who belongs to another species can enlarge your soul in surprising ways. In these pages you'll meet animals who changed my life by the briefest of meetings. You'll meet others who became members of my family. Some are dogs who shared our home. One's a pig who lived in our barn. Three are huge flightless birds, two are tree kangaroos, and there's also a spider, a weasel, and an octopus.

I am still learning how to be a good creature. Though I try earnestly, I often fail. But I am having a great life trying—a life exploring this sweet green world—and returning to a home where I am blessed with a multispecies family offering me comfort and joy beyond my wildest dreams. I often wish I could go back in time and tell my young, anxious self that my dreams weren't in vain and my sorrows weren't permanent. I can't do that, but I can do something better. I can tell you that teachers are all around to help you: with four legs or two or eight or even none; some with internal skeletons, some without. All you have to do is recognize them as teachers and be ready to hear their truths.

Sy Montgomery

CHAPTER 1
MOLLY

*A*S USUAL, WHEN I WAS NOT IN CLASS AT ELEMEN-tary school, we were together. Molly—our Scottish terrier—and I were doing sentinel duty on the spacious, crew-cut lawn of the general's house, Quarters 225, Fort Hamilton, Brooklyn, New York. Rather, Molly was keeping watch, and I was watching her.

Unfortunately for a Scottie, bred to hunt down foxes and badgers, far too little prey was to be found on the orderly and efficient army base. Every inch was strictly manicured, and wild animals were not tolerated. Still, because Molly did find the occasional squirrel to chase—and because, though we lived there, the home was not ours but the U.S. Army's, we couldn't put up a fence—she was chained to a sturdy, corkscrewing stake driven deep into the ground. I watched her scan the area with her wet black nose and her pricked, swiveling ears—longing, longing, as I did daily, to smell and hear as she did the invisible comings and goings of distant animals.

And then she was off like a furry cannonball.

In an instant, she had ripped the foot-and-a-half-long stake from the ground and was dragging it and her chain behind her as she charged, snarling with gleeful fury, through the yew bushes in front of the single-story brick house. Quickly I glimpsed what she was chasing: a rabbit!

I leapt to my feet. I had never seen a wild rabbit before. Nobody had ever heard of a wild rabbit on Fort Hamilton! I wanted a closer look. But Molly had chased the rabbit around to the front of the house, and my two, weak, second-grader's feet, imprisoned in their patent leather Mary Janes, couldn't carry me nearly as fast as her four, clawed, fully mature paws.

A Scottish terrier's fierce, deep voice is too commanding to be ignored. Soon, out from our quarters came my mother and one of the enlisted men who had been assigned to help keep the general's house tidy. A forest of legs exploded around me as the adults zigzagged after our furious terrier. But of course they couldn't catch her. By this time Molly had broken free of the chain and left the stake behind. There was no stopping her. Whether she caught the rabbit or not, she'd be out for hours, perhaps till after dark. She'd come back, signaling at the door to be let in with a single, summoning woof, only when she was good and ready.

Though I wished I could have run after her, it wouldn't have been to stop her. I wanted to go *with* her. I wanted to see the rabbit again. I wanted to learn the smells around the post at night. I wanted to meet other dogs and wrestle and chase them, to poke my nose into holes and smell who lived there, to discover treasures hidden in the dirt.

Many young girls worship their older sisters. I was no exception. But my older sister was a dog, and I—standing there helplessly in the frilly dress and lacy socks in which my mother had dressed me—wanted to be just like her: Fierce. Feral. Unstoppable.

✧

I WAS NEVER, MY MOTHER TOLD ME, A "NORMAL" CHILD.

As evidence, she cited the day she and my father first took me to the zoo. I had just begun to walk, and, breaking free of my parents' hands, toddled to my chosen destination:

inside the pen housing some of the largest and most dangerous animals in the institution. The hippos must have gazed
upon me benignly rather than biting me in half, as these three-
thousand-pound animals are prone to do, or stepping on me.
Because somehow my parents got me out of there unscathed.
My mother, however, never completely recovered from the
incident.

I was always drawn to animals—far more than I was ever
attracted to other children, or adult humans, or dolls. I preferred watching my two goldfish, Goldie and Blackie, and
playing with my beloved but ill-fated turtle, Ms. Yellow Eyes.
(My mother was from the South, and long before feminism,
I learned from her the southern habit of bestowing on all females the honorific Ms.) Like most pet turtles in the 1950s,
Ms. Yellow Eyes suffered from improper diet and died when
her shell got soft. To console me, my mother gave me a baby
doll, but I ignored it. When my father returned from a trip to
South America and brought me back a stuffed baby caiman,
a type of crocodile, I dressed it in the baby doll's clothing and
pushed it around in the doll's pram.

An only child, I never yearned for siblings. I didn't need
other kids around. Most children were loud and wiggly. They

wouldn't stay still long enough to watch a bumblebee. They ran and scattered the pigeons strutting on the sidewalk.

With rare exceptions, adult humans were not particularly memorable either. I would stare blankly at an adult I had seen many times, unable to place them, unless one of my parents could remind me of their pet. (For example, "They're the ones with Brandy." Brandy was a miniature longhaired dachshund with red hair who loved to snuggle with me in my bed while the adults continued to enjoy their party after I was tucked in. I still can't remember his people's names or recall their faces.) One of the few petless humans I loved was my "uncle" Jack, not really an uncle, but a colonel, a friend of my father's, who would draw pictures of pinto ponies for me. I would carefully color in the spots while he and my father played chess.

When my language skills had grown robust enough to discuss such matters, I announced to my parents that I was really a horse. I galloped around the house neighing and tossing my head. My father agreed to call me "Pony." But my elegant and socially ambitious mother, wishing that her little girl had the good sense to pretend she was a princess or a fairy, was worried. She feared that I was mentally defective.

The army pediatrician assured her the pony phase would

wear off. It did—but only when I revealed that now I was really a dog.

From my perspective, this presented only one problem. While my parents and their friends were eager to show me how to be a little girl, there was nobody around who could show me how to be a dog. Until I was three and my short life's ambition was realized with the arrival of Molly.

A SCOTTISH TERRIER PUPPY IS "BOLD AND JAUNTY," SAY breed websites, as well as notably "active and willful." A Scottie's characteristic traits of toughness and independence are evident even from infancy. An ancient breed concocted by thrifty Scots to keep vermin from bothering their livestock, these small black dogs are Highland warriors. They're strong and brave enough to subdue foxes and badgers, and smart enough to capably work independent of their owners and outwit wild intruders. Standing a mere ten inches tall and weighing only about twenty pounds, Scotties "have all the compactness of a small dog and all the valor of a big one," the critic and author Dorothy Parker wrote. "And," she added, "they are so exceedingly sturdy that it is proverbial that the only fatal thing to them is being run over by an automobile—in which case, the car itself knows it has been in a fight." A Scottie puppy is like a terrible two-year-old tot on steroids and gifted with an almost unnatural indestructibility.

But, despite our shared toddlerhood, tough, feisty little Molly was exactly my opposite.

Something bad happened to me once I turned two, after my family moved back to the States from Germany, where I'd been born. In Germany, we'd had a nanny, but now I was my mother's responsibility. My mother would later tell me that I contracted a very rare case of early childhood mononucleosis. But my father's sister thought this was a lie, and indeed, many years later, I found no note of this diagnosis in my army medical records. My aunt was convinced I had been smothered, shaken violently, or both, probably repeatedly. Evidently I cried a lot. Even many years later, when I was a teenager, my mother still complained bitterly to her friends about how my crying often ruined her cocktail hour. Her evening martinis were the best part of her day. They must have eased her loneliness when my father was away, leaving her alone with a howling baby.

Whatever happened to me, for many months afterward, I wouldn't play or talk. I refused to eat. I turned three, and still I hadn't grown.

My condition must have distressed both my parents. My mother bought a little bowl with animals at the bottom, which I could see only if I finished my cereal. She cut my toast into animal shapes with cookie cutters; my father tried to tempt me with milkshakes (into which he had clandestinely slipped a raw egg). Their desperation over my failing health may have been what prompted them to consider adopting a puppy.

Today, dog trainers and parenting coaches would have warned against it. Dog trainers agree that Scotties, while wonderful dogs, are not a good match for small children. Toddlers might step on toes or clutch at a tail, and Scotties won't put up with this. They're apt to bite, and their jaws and teeth are as big as an Airedale's. Scotties are exceptionally loyal, but they are also considered the fiercest of the terriers. And today most experts caution against getting even the most docile and patient of dog breeds till a child is six or even seven.

But of course, nobody knew any of that then—so the glamorous Cuban émigrée whom I knew as Aunt Grace gave us one of her three precious puppies.

Aunt Grace was not really my aunt, and her husband, whom I grew up calling Uncle Clyde, was not really my uncle. Uncle Clyde was my father's best friend, but Aunt Grace was my mother's rival. Aunt Grace wore her waist-length jet-black hair pinned into elaborate twists, custom-tailored dresses that featured plunging necklines and slit skirts, black eyeliner, crimson lipstick, and high heels. My mother considered her a showoff. "What color dress do you think Aunt Grace wore to the vet when she took the puppies in for their vaccinations?" she once asked me.

"Black?" I guessed. Personally, I would have wanted to look as similar as possible to the rest of the family. "No," my mother corrected me—"white!" The puppies would show up better that way.

It must have been soon after that vet visit that Molly came to live with us. And though nothing in my short life could have possibly matched the glory of that day, alas—whether because of my illness or injury, or because I was just too young—any memory of that life-changing moment is lost to me.

But its effect was soon obvious.

Not long after she joined us, my parents took a black-and-white photo of Molly and me—one that my mother would later send as the family's holiday greeting card the Christmas two months before I'd turn four. Though my short, puffy sleeves show the season is summer, Christmas stockings hang by the fireplace and a mechanical Santa doll stands beside me on the brick floor, ready to ring a brass bell. Like all my mother's Christmas card compositions, it was a set-up shot. But Molly's and my elated expressions are genuine.

"Molly's got a Daddy sock!"

Like most puppies, Molly loved to steal, and she especially loved to seize my father's black dress socks, the ones he wore to work with his general's uniform. When Molly would steal them, far from tattling on her, I would eagerly announce to the household the spectacle that would follow. It always amused my dog-loving father. Having routed the sock from its usual lair in the bedroom hamper, or sometimes from where it was hiding in the toe of a shoe, Molly would race into the living room, growling ferociously, and then shake the sock with single-minded, delighted fury. There was no getting the sock back until Molly was certain that she had broken its neck.

As a puppy, Molly didn't chew things. She killed them. Sure, she liked rawhides and bones, but she was after something utterly different when she attacked my father's socks. Though I can't remember her ever actually slaying any animal, she imagined objects to be alive, and then imagined herself killing them.

She loved to destroy balls. Small ones didn't interest her. She didn't fetch. With explosive intensity, she chased large, air-filled plastic spheres—soccer balls, kick balls, dodge balls—and she bested them all. I would walk her on leash from our quarters down to the army post's tennis courts early in the morning, before the adults would occupy the space, to roll one of these balls for her. With her deep-throated growls reverberating in my chest, I'd watch her tear across the clay surface of the court as the ball struggled to stay ahead of her nose. But she would always corner it; once she punctured its lungs with her long white canines, the ball would deflate enough so she could get the entire thing in her strong jaws and shake it into oblivion. When it was dead she let me pick it up and examine it. The thing looked as if it had been punctured by ice picks. A small dog had done this with her *face*. I was impressed early on that Molly was a powerful being, worthy of deep respect.

I KNEW THERE WAS A VIVID, GREEN, BREATHING WORLD OUT THERE, BUSTLING WITH THE BUSY LIVES OF BIRDS AND INSECTS, TURTLES AND FISH, RABBITS AND DEER.

Apparently others on the post recognized this too. When Molly was older, after we gave up on the stake and chain, she would frequently go out at night alone. Folks on the post got to know her. On one of her nightly jaunts, she visited the Women's Auxiliary Army Corps barracks. (Women were not integrated with the male army until 1978.) A number of the women were outside that night, and word got back to us the next day that when they saw Molly trotting by, they stood in line, allowed her to sniff them, and then saluted her as she continued on her way.

The story could well be apocryphal. Or it could be the WAACs really saluted her only because she was the general's dog. It could also be that these strong, brave women saw and respected this little female dog's independence and spunk. An earlier general had recognized this quality too in his Scotties. The commander of the Scottish army, Major General George Douglas, also known as the Earl of Dumbarton, had a pack of distinguished Scottish terriers in the nineteenth century whom he nicknamed "the Diehards." His Scotties inspired him to name his favorite regiment, the Royal Scots, after them: "Dumbarton's Diehards."

With typical Scottie self-reliance, Molly didn't need people to tell her what to do. She wouldn't come when we called her in at night. Eventually my parents figured out we could blink the front porch lights on and off to signal that we would *like* her to come home. It was merely a suggestion—the way my father felt about traffic lights (he called a red light "just a suggestion"). Molly would come home when she felt like it.

This bothered me not at all. I certainly didn't expect her to obey *me*. Why should she? By the time I was five, she was only two—but she, by then, was a full adult. I considered her not only my superior, but my role model. I did not even realize that my view of our relationship wasn't endorsed by other humans—until my mother set out to tame us both.

THE VERY CHARACTERISTICS THAT MAKE SCOTTIES special—independence and tenacity—also make them difficult to train. One trainer's website noted that Scotties' famous stubbornness and self-reliance "tend to make them think obedience is optional."

Yet, incredibly, while our Molly was running loose and destroying toys and clothing, my glamorous Aunt Grace managed to train *her* Scotties to say their prayers and play the piano.

Aunt Grace had purchased a squat black child's toy piano, like the kind Schroeder plays in the *Peanuts* cartoon. She would call Mac, Molly's brother, into the living room. "Play the piano!" she would urge with great verve. The dog, sitting in front of the plastic keyboard, would mash first one set of keys, then another, alternating paws. I was also learning piano at the time and was impressed that Mac could play with both hands before I could.

Next Aunt Grace would wow her guests with her Scotties' piety. A large pale blue upholstered footstool would serve as their dinner table, set with two matching blue placemats ready to receive two dog dishes. While Aunt Grace held their shiny aluminum bowls brimming with food, Mac and his mother, Ginny, would sit up, side by side. Aunt Grace set the bowls down. "Say your prayers!" she'd urge, and the Scotties would place their paws at the edge of the "dining table" in front of them, bow their heads, and tuck their snouts beneath their paws. They'd hold this position until Aunt Grace signaled it was time to eat.

This was impressive, and impressing one's peers was very important in army high society. My mother was no dog trainer —though as a child in Arkansas, she'd had a beloved little beagle mix named Flip, who was tragically run over by a car—but she was a skilled seamstress. So she set out to best her glamorous rival. Our dog might not be able to perform like a person, but she could dress like one.

Though the Scottie's hard, wiry coat was bred for weather resistance, my mother began to sew little coats for Molly. She had coats for both summer and winter wear. A tartan plaid would have been nice, but my mother went for pastels— Molly was female, after all, and my mother felt she should dress the part. Then she turned her attention to Molly's furniture. Mac had a piano in Aunt Grace's living room. Molly would not be outdone. My mother bought a canopy bed for Molly, which was headquartered between the kitchen and the living room, for which she created covers, a pillow, and of course a canopy in royal red satin, with ruffles all around.

My own dresses began to sprout more ruffles too as my mother tried, with increasing fervor, to make me at least look like the dainty little girl she'd always wanted. At the private school in Brooklyn, girls did not wear slacks, and in fact I didn't own any jeans until we moved and I entered public school in fifth grade. I was strictly admonished not to get my clothes dirty, to the point that in kindergarten I'd refused to finger-paint even with a smock on—a tale my mother recounted many years later with great pride.

At her featherweight black-and-gold Singer sewing machine, my mother created dress after pretty dress for me, often in fabric that would match one of her own. Her most dazzling achievement was the outfit she made for me for an elementary school play, in which I, because I was always shorter than all the other kids in my class, played Little Bo Peep. The costume, all pink and white, with eyelet lace and an embroidered bonnet, was so spectacular that the audience gasped when I stepped on stage.

But as my mother valued girly-ness, I revered doggy-ness. I was entranced by Molly's otherworldly powers. She could hear my father's approaching staff car long before it arrived in the driveway. She could smell an opened can of Ken-L Ration from the moment my mother took it out of the refrigerator. She could see in the dark.

Could I acquire such superpowers, I wondered? On TV, cartoon characters could walk through walls like Casper the Friendly Ghost and fly in rocket ships like on *Space Angel*. But here was a being who really did have more-than-human genius, and as a small child I pledged myself her acolyte.

No spot on her body eluded my fascinated scrutiny, from the sandy bumps on her long pink tongue to the way her anus seemed to bloom when she hunched to defecate. I followed avidly every swivel and fold of her ears, every twitch and flare of her rubbery nose. Everything about Molly was perfect.

There were many differences between Molly and me, besides the most obvious ones. Her nostrils were shaped like commas. Mine were simple holes. Her ears were not just mobile, unlike my stationary ones, but inside them, I could see they housed mysterious cartilaginous structures unlike my own. But these differences, I decided, were not insurmountable. Maybe I could still be like her. If only I could learn her doggy secrets! I remember spending hours lying on the floor, my head resting on my arm, inches from her face, watching her sleep, trying to absorb her scent, her breath, her dreams.

In my fantasies—elaborate daydreams I nurtured for years—Molly and I would run away from home together.

We'd live in the woods. We'd lap water from clear streams. We'd find food in the forest, and shelter in a hollow tree. All the other animals would know us, and we would know them. We'd spend our days watching, sniffing, digging, exploring. She would teach me all about the world—the *real* world, outside the post, away from school, far from asphalt and brick and concrete. With her at my side, I could learn the secrets of wild animals.

Even though we lived on an army base, and later in the tame suburbs, I knew there was a vivid, green, breathing world out there, bustling with the busy lives of birds and insects, turtles and fish, rabbits and deer. I knew it from books and from TV shows like *Wild Kingdom* and *The Undersea World of Jacques Cousteau*—but I *believed* it because Molly could hear it and smell it. The real world, the world I already loved, was just out of my ordinary human sensory range. For now. But one day, I knew, we'd escape and go there, to the wild places, where Molly would at last share with me her animal powers.

CHAPTER 2
BALD THROAT, BLACK HEAD, AND KNACKERED LEG

*A*LONE WITH THE WIND AND THE DRY, WINTERING scrub, I was squatting in a sea of thorny ground cover in middle of the Australian Outback. Then, suddenly, I knew somebody was there.

I was twenty-six, five years out of college, and literally half a world away from home—which most recently had been New Jersey, where I'd worked for five years as a science and environmental reporter for a daily newspaper. But now, I was sampling small plants for a graduate student's botanical survey. The only sound, other than my knife cutting the stems, was the wind blowing through the low bushes and stunted eucalyptus trees called mallee—until something jerked my mind away from my work. I looked up to see three giant birds, each as tall as a man, strolling casually through the brown grass, not fifteen feet away from me.

They were emus. Nearly six feet tall, typically seventy-five pounds, these flightless birds stand beside the kangaroo on Australia's coat of arms as a symbol of this otherworldly continent at the bottom of the globe. Emus seem part bird and part mammal, with a little dinosaur thrown in. Shaggy, twin-shafted brown feathers hang from the rounded torso like hair. A long black neck periscopes up from the body, ending in a gooselike beak. The wings are mere stumps, and stick out from the body like comical afterthoughts. But on their strong, backwards-bending legs, emus can run forty miles an hour—and sever fencing wire, or break a neck, with a single kick.

At the sight of them, a shock leapt from the top of my head down my spine. I'd never been so close to this large a wild animal before—much less while alone, on a foreign continent. I was not so much afraid as I was dazzled. I froze, caught by their grace and power and strangeness, as they lifted their long, scaly legs and folded their huge dinosaurian toes, then set them down again. Balletically dipping their necks into an S-shape as they picked at the grass, they walked past me, and then over the ridge. Finally their haystack-like bodies blended into the brown, rounded forms of the wintering bushes, and were gone.

After they left, I felt a shift in my psyche. But I had no idea that I had just caught the first glimpse of a life farther off the beaten path than I had ever imagined. I could not have known it then, but these strange giant birds would grant me the destiny Molly had inspired, and they would repay me a millionfold for my first act of true bravery: leaving all that I loved behind.

ALMOST EVERYONE HAD THOUGHT I WAS CRAZY WHEN I'D left the United States. My mother had been horrified, though my father assured her the move would get "the travel bug" out of my system. I'd quit my well-paying job, one I had parlayed from a cub reporter covering nine rural towns to the beat I had hoped for while I was a college journalism student. Within a year of graduating from university, having triple majored in journalism, French, and psychology, I was covering science, environment, and medicine in a state with urgent environmental issues to investigate and more scientists and engineers per capita than any other in the nation.

I often worked fourteen-hour days and weekends and was

hungry for more. My work was rewarded with awards, raises, and freedom. Surrounded with talented editors, smart colleagues, and good friends, I lived in a little cabin in the woods with five ferrets, two lovebirds, and the man I loved, Howard Mansfield, a brilliant writer whom I'd met in college. I was happy.

And then came a gift that changed my life. After I had worked five years at the *Courier-News,* my father, now retired from the army and ever my champion, gave me a plane ticket to Australia. I'd always wanted to visit. Sculpted by isolation, Australia's animals outpace the imagination. Instead of antelopes or deer trotting on four feet, kangaroos bounce about on two, carrying babies in belly pockets. Echidnas, quill-covered mammals who lay eggs, lick up ants with whiplike ribbons of sticky tongue. Beaver-tailed duck-billed platypuses defend themselves with poison spines at the ankles of their webbed feet.

I wanted to do more than just see these animals. I wanted to study, and, if possible, help the creatures from whom I was learning. I discovered an organization that paired paying laymen with scientific and conservation projects around the world. Earthwatch, a nonprofit based in Massachusetts, offered "citizen science" expeditions geared to a working person's schedule. Each lasted only a few weeks. I signed up for a project in the state of South Australia, assisting Dr. Pamela Parker, a conservation biologist at Chicago's Brookfield Zoo, with a study of the endangered southern hairy-nosed wombat at Brookfield Conservation Park, a two-hour drive from the city of Adelaide.

We seldom saw the wombats. Looking rather like koalas but living in holes instead of trees, the wombats were shy and spent much of their time in the extensive tunnels they'd dug in the rock-hard soil. We would see them at a distance, though, basking in the afternoon sunlight on their burrow mounds. Occasionally we caught them and measured them, but mostly we surveyed their habitat, mapped their burrows, and counted their desert-dry, squareish scats in an effort to estimate their numbers. But we did see kangaroos every day, and they never stopped astounding me. Every creature, plant or animal, in the study area opened a new world, from the fist-size lycosid spider who often appeared inside my tent at night, to the twisted acacia trees that somehow survived in the dry red soil. At night, we cooked our food over eucalypt-scented campfires. We slept in tents pitched beneath scrubby Outback trees. In the mornings we watched sunrises streaked with flocks of gray-and-pink parrots. Here was a taste of the dream I had cherished as a child: living in the wild, discovering the animals' secrets.

I worked so hard and so earnestly that at the end of the two weeks, as I faced my return to the United States and my job, Dr. Parker made me an offer. She couldn't hire me as a research assistant. And once I went home, she couldn't pay my airfare to come back to Australia. But if I wanted to conduct independent research on any of the animals living at Brookfield Conservation Park, she would let me stay at her camp and share her food.

So I came home—only to quit my job and move to a tent in the Outback.

THERE WAS ONE BIG DIFFERENCE BETWEEN MY DREAM AS A child of living in the wild woods and moving to the mallee scrub of Australia. In my childhood fantasies, I'd had my mentor with me to show me the way. But of course, Molly was long gone. She'd died peacefully as she slept, in her red canopy bed, when I was a junior in high school. Who now would lead me, a mere human, lonely, disoriented, and inexperienced, into the land of unknown animal powers?

I had no idea what I would study. So I began by assisting other people with their work—for example, taking plant samples for the grad student I was helping the first day I saw the emus. There were usually only six researchers in camp at a time. Sometimes I helped another woman look for evidence of introduced foxes. One day, several of us were tearing down barbed-wire fences left over from when the park had been a ranch. We were cannibalizing the fence posts to mark wombat warrens for Dr. Parker's study when I saw the three emus again.

They arrived noiselessly at a corner of the park about five hundred yards from us. They appeared to be picking at a low, bird-nest-like clot of mistletoe in a eucalyptus tree. Again, the shock stung the top of my head, like a laser bolt. *Pay attention!*

We approached them with cameras and binoculars, ducking behind bushes in an attempt to hide, advancing only when we imagined they weren't looking. But emus are always looking—the average bird's eyesight is many times better than a human's. We were within a hundred yards of them when one pulled himself up to his full height, black neck upstretched, and advanced straight toward us. At about twenty-five yards, the bold bird turned and ran. I noticed he also raised his tail and excreted a sizable watery mass. Thereafter, the three emus ignored us and strolled off over a ridge.

I searched out the poop and found it was studded with green striated seeds. Mistletoe seeds! There and then, I knew what I would study. Are emus important dispersers of seeds? What species do they eat? Do emu droppings help seeds germinate better?

I spent my days roaming the Outback in search of "emu pies." For me, they were as precious, and potentially informative, as the discarded fuel tanks from an alien's space ship. I'd gather them up, schlep them back to camp in bags, and try to identify the seeds I'd find. I'd then return half the seeds to the excrement from which they came and place the other half on a wet paper towel and see if one group grew better than the other.

At the close of one particularly sunny day, I paused to sit and rest on a fallen log. I was watching meat ants crawl over my boots, feeling happy and free. Now I had a scientific purpose to my wanderings.

When I looked up from the ants, I saw the emus again, grazing. I ducked behind a bush, hoping to be able to watch them longer, unseen—but they had already seen me. One began walking straight toward me. He came within twenty-five yards and *ran,* straight across my line of vision, and then stopped. The other two advanced and did the exact same thing. The three stood, as if waiting.

Was this a challenge? An invitation? A test? They must have wondered: Was I dangerous? Would I chase them? If I did, how fast could I run?

Trying to hide, I realized, was futile. I remembered that Jane Goodall, whose famous chimp studies chronicled in *National Geographic* made her one my childhood heroines, had come to the same conclusion. She didn't try to steal glimpses of her study animals. Instead, she offered her presence, humbly and openly, until the chimps felt comfortable with her.

So thereafter, I dressed in exactly the same clothes every day: my father's old green army jacket, blue jeans, red kerchief. I wanted to reassure the birds: It's only me; I'm harmless. I reckoned they could see me long before I could see them.

After that day, I began to encounter them more often. Soon I could find them almost every day. And within a few weeks, I could follow them at fifteen feet—close enough to see their eyes clearly, mahogany irises with pupils black as holes; close enough to see the shafts of their feathers; close enough to see the veins on the leaves of the plants they ate.

I could easily tell them apart. One had a long scar on his right leg. I named him Knackered Leg. (*Knackered* is Australian slang I'd learned from a zookeeper. It means "messed up" and is more impolite than I then realized.) His injury might have been the reason he sat down most often of the three. Black Head seemed to be the most forward emu of the group, and took the lead most often. It was surely he who approached us straight on during my second meeting with them. Bald Throat had a whitish patch on his throat where the black feathers were sparse. He seemed skittish. When the wind would blow or a car would approach, he'd be the first to run.

I referred to the three as "he" for no anatomical reason. There is no way humans can sex live emus until someone lays an egg. But I couldn't think of these marvelous individuals as *it*s. I knew, though, that they were not quite adult, because they lacked the turquoise neck patches that adorn the mature birds. And they were surely siblings, having left their father's care (the male incubates the greenish-black eggs and takes care of the up to twenty chicks who hatch) only weeks or months earlier. Like me, they were just starting to explore their world.

What do they do all day? I wondered. On one of our rare trips to Adelaide, I'd visited the university library. Nobody had published a scientific paper describing the behavior of a group of wild emus before. So, while I continued the seed germination experiments (and yes, seeds did germinate more quickly after passing through an emu's gut), chronicling the birds' daily lives became the new focus of my work.

I developed a checklist of behaviors: walk, run, sit, graze, browse, groom, and so on. I took inventory of what each emu was doing at thirty-second intervals for half an hour. Then I'd switch to a narrative description for the next half-hour. Back and forth I'd go, between methods, from the moment I found them each day till the moment they outpaced me and left, which they invariably did. I never tried to run after them—it would have been pointless—but I always hated to see them go.

Even the most mundane of their activities held me riveted. Watching them sit was a major discovery. First they dropped to their "knees"—what looks like a bird's knee is more analogous to a person's ankle—then, to my surprise, to their chests! I hadn't realized they had two different sitting positions. Watching them rise was equally surprising. To stand, they jerked forward, using neck and chest to propel them to a kneeling position, and then made a squatting leap to their feet.

Seeing them drink was also unexpected—so much so that I hadn't included it as a behavior on the checklist. It was weeks before I saw them kneel to scoop up beak-fulls from a puddle in the road after a rare Outback rain. Many desert animals get all their moisture from their food and don't drink, and I hadn't expected to see it.

Watching them preen was also revelatory, and deeply satisfying. I loved seeing them groom their stringy brown feathers. As their beaks combed roughly through the barbules of their feathers, it recalled for me sunny, sofa-bound afternoons with my grandmother brushing my hair. I imagined how good it felt for them. I found myself sharing their pleasure in this calming, intimate act.

On gusty days when the wind would toss their feathers, they would dance, throwing their neck to the sky, splashing the air with their strong feet. I had the feeling that they did this for pure joy. They also had a sense of humor. One day I watched them approach the ranger's dog, tied on a chain outside his house. The dog barked hysterically, but bold Black Head, head and shoulders raised high, continued approaching the straining animal head-on. Once Black Head was within twenty feet, he raised his wing stumps forward, hurled his neck upward, and leapt into the air with both feet kicking, repeating the behavior for perhaps forty seconds. Soon the other two joined him, and the dog went absolutely wild. The emus then raced off across the dog's line of vision for about three hundred yards, before sitting down abruptly to preen— as if to congratulate themselves on the success of their prank. I admired shy Bald Throat and injured Knackered Leg for their bravery, and realized that their leader, Black Head, must have given them great confidence to be able to tease a predator.

The three were quite aware of themselves as a group. Whenever one would stray too far from the others, he would look up, assess the situation, and run or trot to close the distance between them to twenty-five yards or so. After a month, I could sometimes get within five feet of Black Head and within ten feet of the others.

I FROZE, CAUGHT
BY THEIR GRACE
AND POWER AND
STRANGENESS.

I, too, looked to Black Head for guidance. If I could catch his eye, with a glance I'd try to assess whether he was happy with me following everyone or not. In a sense, I was asking his permission to follow. And yet in another way, by acknowledging him as the leader of the group, I made him my leader too.

Sometimes, he would look me directly in the eye and hold my gaze. Though in dirty clothes, my uncombed hair matting like the fur on a stray dog, when bathed in the sight of this giant, alien flightless bird, I felt beautiful for the first time in my life.

AT DUSK, THEY ALWAYS SEEMED MORE NERVOUS. ANY QUICK movement—the sight of a car in the distance, a hopping kangaroo, or a tent blowing away (once it was mine)—would send them running. Knackered Leg, after all, had an injury, and an injured animal, even a strong one like an emu, must always be on guard. But it was Bald Throat who was always first to run, and once the other two took off after him, I could never hope to catch up.

Each night as I huddled in my sleeping bag, I wondered where the emus slept. Or did they merely rest? Did one stay awake as a sentry? Did they kneel or sit, or stand—perhaps on one leg, like cold chickadees at home? Did they tuck their black heads beneath their wing stumps?

Some mornings, I got up at four a.m. to see if I could find them sleeping. I never did. But one evening, I followed them and they did not run. It was nearly dark when they sat down, all facing the same direction beneath four stunted eucalypt that formed a canopy under the orange and purple sky. I sat also, so happy to be with them. But as dark gathered around us, I realized I was taking no data. I turned on my flashlight to note the time, and they leapt to their feet and ran away.

Day after blissful day I followed them. I accumulated thousands of pages of data. I felt I was doing something useful for science. Eventually, I would crunch these numbers and figure out what percentage of time they spent strolling, grazing, browsing, grooming—something no one had ever done before.

When I went on a fossil dig elsewhere that I'd committed to help with, I made sure I trained a volunteer to follow the emus and take data in my absence. She seemed competent and determined. But would she miss things? The dig was fascinating, but I was consumed with worry about the study, and I left a day early.

I returned to find my volunteer had filled more than a hundred sheets of data and was following the emus just fine. I just glanced at the sheets before I left to find the emus myself. It was dusk, windy and raining, and the birds were jittery, jogging, then running, as they often were in this weather. I broke my own rule and tried to run after them, but they disappeared into the darkening storm. As the rain turned to hail, I threw myself into a Gigera bush and wept.

It wasn't the data on these emus I wanted, I realized. I simply wanted to be with them.

✧

SIX MONTHS IS A LONG TIME TO WORK WITHOUT PAY. I HAD always planned after half a year to return to the States. I'd soon pack up my tent and move to a carriage house that Howard had rented for us in a small New Hampshire town. Five days before I was to leave the park, I found the emus sitting near a favored patch of wild mustard. Knackered Leg looked up at my approach, and then the two other heads rose and turned to look at me. I think they were sitting because the wind was strong enough to knock them over. I lay on my belly to minimize its force as they snatched mouthfuls of wild mustard and groomed themselves. The wind died down, and by noon, we were moving again, strolling together toward the spot where I had first seen them. We crossed the sea of spiky plants. We crossed the reserve's main track. A truck passed, but they didn't startle. I got within three feet of Black Head and held his gaze. Then I looked to Bald Throat and Knackered Leg. Never before had I seen the three so calm. I thought, *Tonight?*

The night would be moonless. Would I finally get to see them sleep?

Even at dusk, no one jogged. No one ran. We entered an area of thick bush I'd not visited before. In the darkening brush I could see only Knackered Leg, five feet away. His injury had healed impressively over the months we had known each other, but I always felt a special tenderness toward him, and his trust in letting me get so close in the dark meant a great deal to me. I could hear Bald Throat and Black Head's footsteps, pacing steadily.

I couldn't see my data sheet or my watch. Even the stars were obscured by clouds. I heard the birds sit down. *Thump*— to their knees. *Thump*—to their chests. I could hear, but not see, what they were doing: the scuffle of shifting their great armored feet beneath them, the purr of feathers being combed through their bills. And then, silence. I no longer even cared about the data. What mattered was it was dark and safe, and we were together as they slept.

THE DAY BEFORE I LEFT, I FOLLOWED THEM FROM DAWN TO dark. As eager as I was to return to Howard, as much as I looked forward to seeing my ferrets and lovebirds and friends again, I was heartbroken at the thought of leaving the emus. I wished I could convey to them what they had given me: Peace as soothing as the calm they feel when they groom their feathers. Joy as spirited as their dance in the wind. Satisfaction as fulfilling as a bellyful of mistletoe.

I learned a great deal in the Outback, from how to conduct a behavioral study to how to urinate outdoors without peeing on my shoe. After living in the bush for six months, I knew I could never return to scrambling into pantyhose to work in an office or answering to a boss. Now I knew I would spend the rest of my life writing about animals, going wherever their stories would take me. Molly, who had saved my life, had shown me my destiny. The emus, on their tall, impossibly backwards-bending legs, had let me stroll with them for the first steps along the path.

The data I'd amassed on the emus was new, but not particularly surprising. I didn't discover the birds using tools or waging war against other emu groups, the way Jane Goodall found with her chimps. But in my last hours with the emus, I realized something that would prove, to me as a writer, very important. To begin to understand the life of any animal demands not only curiosity, not only skill, and not only intellect. I saw that I would also need to summon the bond I had forged with Molly. I would need to open not only my mind, but also my heart.

CHAPTER 3

CHRISTOPHER HOGWOOD

*H*OWARD AND I THRIVED IN NEW HAMPSHIRE. WE loved its woods and wetlands, its short, intense summers, flaming fall foliage, and winters blanketed with sparkly snow. We both found freelance work: magazine articles on giant insects and possums took me to New Zealand, I researched animal language studies in Hawaii and California, and I wrote a nature column for the *Boston Globe*. Howard wrote regularly for *Yankee, Historic Preservation, American Heritage,* and various newspapers. We became fast friends with the older couple from whom we rented our little carriage house just off Main Street in the small town of New Ipswich. When our library and files outgrew that small space, we moved to half of a two-family farmhouse on eight acres in Hancock, a smaller town nearby. The place had a brook, a barn, a fenced field.

After a military childhood of frequent moves, I felt like I had finally found a home.

We celebrated the publication of Howard's first book, *Cosmopolis*, about future cities. I landed a contract for my first book—a tribute to my childhood heroines, the primatologists Jane Goodall, Dian Fossey, and Birute Galdikas—which led to research trips to East Africa and Borneo. We got married on a friend's farm, with thirty humans, four horses, three cats, a dog, and a new foal in attendance.

But then, everything went wrong.

The house we lived in went up for sale. The publisher for my book pulled out of the contract. I went to Africa anyway, where at the end of a two-month, three-nation research expedition, Jane Goodall failed to meet me at her remote camp as she had promised, leaving me stranded and, worse, without the scene I needed for my first chapter. Worst of all, my father, my hero, was dying of lung cancer. I felt I was about to lose almost everything—our home, my book, my dad.

It did not seem a good time to be adopting a baby animal of a species we knew almost nothing about. But on a dreary March day, the kind when your spinning tires kick frozen mud all over your car, and the remaining snow looks as appealing as sodden

Kleenex, we nonetheless found ourselves driving back over dirt roads to our precariously temporary home with a shoebox on my lap containing a very sickly black-and-white spotted piglet.

✧

HOWARD HAD BEEN THE ONE WHO'D AGREED TO TAKE THE pig. I'd been in Virginia, caring for my father, when the call came from farmer friends in a nearby town. Their kindly sows produced a record number of piglets that spring, including many runts. The smallest of all was less than half the size of the others. He was sick with every disease in the barn, with runny eyes and worms and diarrhea. They called him "the spotted thing." This runt needed far more TLC than the farmers had time to give. Besides, even if he recovered, nobody would want such a small pig for the freezer, which was the fate of all his littermates. Could we take him?

Normally, Howard wouldn't have even told me about the call. He wouldn't even let me enter the local animal shelter for fear I'd come home with half its population. We no longer had our ferrets, but since we'd moved to Hancock, our lovebirds had been joined by a cockatiel whose owners no longer wanted him, a homeless crimson rosella parrot, and our landlord's affectionate and playful white-and-gray cat. But now Howard was desperate to cheer me up. The best thing he could think of to do the trick was adopt a baby pig.

We named him Christopher Hogwood, after the conductor who founded the Academy of Ancient Music, whose recordings we often enjoyed on New Hampshire Public Radio. We hoped that all the little guy needed was some warmth, some love, and a reprieve from hungry brothers and sisters who pushed him away from the food.

But we had never raised a pig before. In fact, other than the offspring of our ferrets, whose own mothers took care of them, we'd never raised a baby of any kind. We didn't know for sure that Chris would even survive. If he did, we had no idea how large he'd grow. And because most pigs are killed and eaten at the tender age of six months, we had no idea how long he might live.

But the biggest surprise in store was that from the moment the sick piglet came home with us, Christopher Hogwood would begin to heal *me*.

✧

"UNH. UNH! *UNH!*" CHRISTOPHER HOGWOOD WOULD call when his oversize furry ears picked up the sound of my footsteps approaching the barn. He sounded like he couldn't wait to see me. We would both squeal with delight upon contact. I'd push open the temporary gate to his pen we'd made from pallets and string, and sit down in the hay and wood shavings to hand-feed him his breakfast.

Then he'd investigate the lawn with his wondrous nose disk, thoughtfully grunting a running commentary, and when he tired of that we'd go back in the pen and he'd push his surprisingly strong, wet snout into the crook of my arm and we'd snuggle.

With his big, appealing ears—one shell pink, one black—his questing pink nose, and a black spot over one eye like Spuds MacKenzie, the dog in a popular beer commercial, Christopher was about the most adorable baby I had ever seen. He was extra cute because he was so little. Each hoof was small enough to stand on a quarter. Imagine an entire pig who could fit in a shoebox! But while his body was tiny, his personality was huge. He was cheerful, inquisitive, and a great communicator. Quickly we learned to decode his desires: "Unh. Unh! UNH!" meant "Come here—now!" "Unh?

Unh? Unh?": What's for breakfast? "Unh. Unh. Unh," slow and deep, directed me to rub his belly. ("Unhhhhhh" indicated the spot where it felt best.) A squeal of "Ree!" expressed excitement—though a high pitch indicated distress. He had a special greeting grunt for Howard and a slightly higher one for me. He had me wrapped around his cloven hoof. I loved him so much it scared me.

UNFORTUNATELY, THE DELIGHT WITH WHICH I BEHELD MY baby was not shared by my parents when they saw theirs. They were mad at me. I wasn't turning out the way they wanted. They had urged me to train for the army in college. I declined. They had kept a membership for me at both the Army Navy Town Club and Army Navy Country Club in Washington, D.C., hoping I might meet a suitable military man. I never did. The person I chose to spend my life with must have seemed, to them, like the last straw. Howard, with his abundant curly hair and progressive views, could not have possibly seemed less like their vision of a suitable army officer. Plus, he was Jewish;

I was raised Methodist. His family was middle class and liberal while mine was wealthy and conservative. In a venomous letter that arrived the week after our wedding, my father had formally disowned me, likening me to the snake in Shakespeare's *Hamlet:* "the serpent that did sting thy father's life." To my parents, I was a different species.

Nonetheless, nearly two years later, when I had heard through my aunt in California that my father was sick, I had immediately boarded a plane to Washington to be by his side at Walter Reed Army Medical Center as he recovered from his first lung surgery. He and my mother were glad I was there, and glad upon my every return. But my husband was never welcome in their home—not even for my father's funeral. Though I was with him when he died, my father never told me he forgave me, and my mother could not accept my living a life so different from their own.

But unlike the case with my human family, the differences between Christopher and me (he a quadruped, me a biped; he having hooves, I lacking hooves entirely, and so on) would not trouble our relationship. He was a pig—and I loved him for it, just as I had loved Molly not despite her being a dog but *because* she was a dog. And as I would soon learn, Christopher would also, with great generosity, accept, and perhaps forgive, that I was only human.

✧

OTHER THAN OUR PHYSICAL DIFFERENCES, THERE WAS AN-other important contrast between me and Christopher. I was shy. He was not. Christopher was an extrovert who loved company—and he sought it by frequently breaking out of his pen. We had secured the makeshift gate to his pen with an elaborate tangle of bungee cords, but Chris, with a pig's high intelligence and flexible nose and lips, managed to dislodge them. He wanted to visit the neighbors.

"There's a pig on our lawn! Is it yours?" I'd get a phone call and rush out the door to retrieve him. Sometimes I'd arrive bed-headed and still in my nightshirt—not optimal for socializing, especially with neighbors I hardly knew. But I was always welcomed, because by the time I arrived, Christopher had already charmed his hosts. I'd show up to find them scratching behind his big ears, rubbing his belly, or feeding him a treat. "He's so cute! He's so friendly!" they'd exclaim. They'd want to know all about him.

Previously, I'd have been at a loss to come up with a subject for conversation. I didn't know about the things it seemed most people talked about—kids, cars, sports, fashion, movies . . . But now, even at parties, which I used to dread, I had something to contribute: how Christopher brilliantly engineered his breakouts; that pigs not only recognize individuals but remember them for years; how Chris loved watermelon rinds but hated onions, and didn't Hoover up his food, but chose each bite with care and precision, lifting each morsel from his bowl delicately with his lips. What were we going to "do" with him? people would ask. "I'm a vegetarian and my husband is Jewish," I'd explain. "We're certainly not going to eat him. But we might send him abroad for university studies . . ." Then we'd invite folks over for what we called "dinner and a show." If they brought their leftovers—stale bagels, extra macaroni and cheese, freezer-burned ice cream—they could watch Christopher eat it. It was always a jolly occasion. Yankees hate waste, and watching Christopher's delight in eating

HE TAUGHT US HOW
TO LOVE. HOW TO LOVE
WHAT LIFE GIVES YOU.
EVEN WHEN LIFE
GIVES YOU SLOPS.

was contagious. Soon, neighbors who had been strangers were friends.

Christopher's timing was perfect, because Howard and I were now landowners in town. Miraculously, we were able to buy the house we lived in. The price came down when the owners discovered the land was just short of eight acres, which made the property one lot and not two. So, anchored to our beloved home by a growing pig, like most young married couples who begin settling down, we decided it was time to enlarge our family.

FIRST CAME THE LADIES. ONE OF MY DEAREST FRIENDS gave us eight hand-raised black sex-link hens as a housewarming present. They looked like a small congregation of nuns—if nuns had cheerful red combs, orange eyes, and scaly yellow feet. They ranged freely around the property, scratching for bugs, murmuring in their lilting chicken voices, racing to greet us when we'd appear, hoping for a treat or squatting before us to be stroked or picked up and petted.

Next came Tess—a classically beautiful black-and-white longhaired border collie with a turbulent past. Bred for herding, the breed is famously independent, emotional, willful, and smart. Howard had always wanted one. But these dogs have a downside: In the absence of sheep and cows, they've been known to resort to herding insects—or school buses. They need constant stimulation. After Tess, when still a pup, had leapt onto a dining room table during a formal dinner, her original owners gave her to an animal rescue near us, run by a locally celebrated "animal lady," Evelyn Naglie. One winter day, Tess was playing with a child who threw a ball into the street in front of an oncoming snowplow. Tess spent nearly a year recovering from multiple surgeries. She was adopted out to yet another family, but had to be returned a year later when the couple lost their house in a recession. She was only two years old when we took her home from Evelyn's, but Tess had already seen a lifetime of pain, loss, and rejection.

Tess was a great athlete who despite her injured leg soared into the air to catch balls and Frisbees. She knew a great deal of English and was relentlessly obedient. But, except for when we were playing her favorite sports (which worked out to be about once an hour), Tess was as wary of people as Chris was outgoing. She didn't pee, poop, or eat without our specifically asking her to do so. She consented to petting, but seemed confused about the point. She didn't bark for weeks, as if she were afraid to use her voice in the house. The first time we invited her up on our bed she looked at us in shocked disbelief. When we patted the covers, obediently she jumped up, but leapt back down again a second later, as if this couldn't possibly be what we wanted.

Tess seemed to be guarding her emotions. But we knew we could change that. Though love could not heal my father's cancer, I'd seen that it *could* save a sick little pig—at one year old, Christopher was now a robust 250 pounds and growing. Surely our love could also redeem the cruelty and sorrow that had haunted our lovely Tess's past.

✧

AFTER THE DOG, JUST LIKE IN THE STORYBOOKS, CAME THE children. But not in the usual way.

I'd never wanted kids of my own, even when I was one. When I discovered, as a child, that I would forever be unable to conceive or bear puppies, I crossed having babies off the list. The Earth was grossly overburdened with humans already.

As Howard and I grew older, most of our friends were

child-free, or they were older and their children were grown up. I didn't regret not having kids in our lives. By the time I turned thirty, I was blessed with a great career, a husband, a home, a cat, a dog, hens, parrots, and a pig who, heading into his second year, topped out at several hundred pounds. In terms of sheer biomass, our family was, in fact, much larger than those of our peers.

By Christopher's second autumn, we had established a new routine. Now he was so large and strong that it was impossible to lead him on a leash. But I could lure him with a bucket of slops—to which the entire neighborhood was now contributing—out to his spacious "Pig Plateau" in the backyard. Tess trotted behind, holding the Frisbee in her mouth. A parade of black hens followed. Once at the Plateau, I'd decant the slops and hook up a long tether to Christopher's specially made harness. I'd talk to him and toss the Frisbee to Tess while he ate. That's what we were doing on an October day when Chris paused in his meal, raised his head, flexed his nose disk, and uttered a grunt. I looked up to see two little blond girls racing toward us as if drawn by a tractor beam.

"It's even cooler than a horse. It's a pig!" the ten-year-old shouted to her younger sister. And then, to me: "Can we pet him?"

I showed how, by rubbing his belly, we could get Chris to flop onto his side. As he grunted with porcine bliss, little hands reached for the softest fur, in back of his ears, as I pointed out the four toes of each of his hooves, his budding tusks, his many nipples. The girls were enthralled.

Christopher, of course, loved the company. Tess enjoyed another set of hands to toss the Frisbee. As the Ladies pecked for slops scraps around us, I learned that the girls would soon be renting the empty house next door. They'd lost their family home in a nasty divorce, and they hadn't been happy about their new house—until now.

From the moment they moved in, Kate, ten, and Jane, seven, were over at our place just about every day. They often brought Christopher sandwiches and apples—which I soon discovered they'd been saving since they left their house in the morning. ("I don't even know why I pack their school lunch," their mom, Lila, later confessed. "I might as well put it directly in Christopher's mouth.") Periodically they decreed that their ice cream was too freezer burned for human consumption and insisted on feeding it to Chris with a spoon. He rose to his back feet, leaning his front trotters on his gate, and held open his now cavernous mouth patiently for each spoonful. Christopher soon greeted the girls with distinctive soft grunts he used for no other visitors.

Kate and Jane also instituted Pig Spa. One spring day, Kate decided that the long ringlet of hair at the tip of Christopher's tail needed to be combed. Then, of course, it needed to be braided. Inevitably for two preteen girls whose house was littered with hair scrunchies and smelled like bubble bath, the effort expanded to an entire beauty regimen for our pig.

We fetched warm buckets of soapy water from the kitchen, and more warm water for the rinse. We added products created for horses to apply to his hooves to make them shine. Grunting his contentment as he lay in his pool of soapy water, Christopher made clear he adored his spa—unless the water was chilly. Then he'd scream like he was being butchered—and we'd race back to the kitchen to fetch a more comfortable bath. He forgave us the instant the warm water touched his skin.

Soon other kids were joining in. Several became regulars. Some favorite neighbors always brought their grandkids when they visited from Iowa. That state has no shortage of pigs, but the kids had never seen one enjoy a spa treatment. A wonderfully cheerful teen, Kelly, would come over after sessions of chemotherapy she needed to fight her cancer. Even though by then Chris was huge and powerful, capable of knocking over a woodpile with a nudge of his nose, he was always absolutely tender with her. Two boys and their family, who also had a home in Massachusetts, refrigerated their leftovers for days and carted them up to Hancock to give to Chris; one day they brought fresh chocolate donuts, which were shared among the kids and the pig. For the first time in my life, I learned how much fun it is to play with children, and looked forward to it every day.

When Kate and Jane's mom began graduate studies for a new career as a therapist, the girls came over right after school and stayed till she came home. Howard went with Jane to her soccer games. I helped Kate with her homework. In the winter, Howard would build a fire in the woodstove next door so Lila wouldn't be cold when she got home. They had us over for dinner. We took the girls on field trips. We went to Christopher's original farm. We visited a nature reserve to release a skunk we'd live-trapped in the henhouse. We overnighted in a tent at an astronomy convention in Vermont. We baked cookies, read books, spent holidays together.

The Ladies realized what had happened before we did. Previously our hens had stuck to the boundaries of our property. Now they started hopping over the stone wall that separated the two backyards and began ranging all over both, as if they owned the place. Somehow, they knew: though we weren't all related, thanks to Christopher Hogwood, our two multi-species households had become one unit.

CHRISTOPHER'S FAME GREW ALONG WITH HIS GIRTH. BY the time he reached his fifth year, his weight topped seven hundred pounds. This was no wonder, because now he was getting food from all corners. Our postmaster saved vegetable scraps for him, and she would put a yellow card in our PO box letting us know we should pick it up. The owner of the cheese shop in the next town would deliver buckets of leftovers—bread crusts, failed soups, the first and last slices of the tomato—right to his pen, usually while singing opera to him. Neighbors brought apples, overgrown zucchini, whey from cheesemaking operations.

His admirers spanned the globe. I carried photos of our mighty pig to impress new friends I would meet on expeditions to study cheetahs and snow leopards and great white sharks. At home, everyone so admired him that he garnered write-in votes at every election.

What was it about Christopher Hogwood that seemed to draw everyone to him? Lila later summed it up this way: "He was a great big Buddha master. He taught us how to love. How to love what life gives you. Even when life gives you slops."

It's true. Chris loved his food. He loved the feel of the warm, soapy water of Pig Spa, the caress of little hands on the soft skin behind his ears. He loved company. No matter who you were—a child or an adult, sick or well, bold or shy, or whether you held out a watermelon rind or a chocolate donut or an empty hand to rub behind his ear—Christopher welcomed you with grunts of good cheer. No wonder everyone adored him.

Studying at the cloven feet of this porcine Buddha every day, I could not help but learn from a master how to revel in and savor this world's abundance: the glow of warm sun on skin, the joy of playing with children. Also, his big heart, and huge body, made my sorrows seem smaller. After a lifetime of moving, Christopher Hogwood helped give me a home. And after my parents had disowned me, out of an assortment of unrelated, unmarried people and animals of many different species, Christopher helped create for me a *real* family—a family made not from genes, not from blood, but from love.

CHAPTER 4

CLARABELLE

CROUCHING IN THE JUNGLE, SWEAT STREAMING FROM my face, I was waiting for a wild animal to rush at me from its hole.

Just hours before, I had landed in French Guiana in northern South America with photographer Nic Bishop. We'd flown over great mosaics of mangrove swamps, then huge climax forest. When you arrive here at night, we'd been told, what strikes you is the darkness. Only 150,000 people live in this country, a land the size of Indiana, and most of it is virgin tropical rainforest. But we had landed in the daytime, and immediately, with Sam Marshall, a biologist from Hiram, Ohio, we had set out to Trésor Réserve after our quarry.

I'd been to jungles on three continents before this to research my books, where I'd become acquainted with lions,

tigers, and bears. But this trip was different. Again, the subjects of our expedition were top predators in their ecosystem, and among the largest and most imposing of their biological family group. But this time, we were looking for spiders.

"Queen of the Jungle" is how Sam described the species we sought: the largest tarantula on Earth, the Goliath birdeater. A big female can weigh a quarter pound. Her head might grow as big around as an apricot, her leg span stretch long enough to cover your face. And if the one Sam had located, in a silk-lined burrow that could stretch for twenty feet, did come rushing out, she might, in fact, cover my face.

The thought was disturbing. For although no tarantula's venom is deadly to a healthy adult human, a bite from a Goliath birdeater's half-inch black fangs will certainly break the skin. And if the spider chooses to inject its venom, which paralyzes its prey, the resulting nausea, sweating, and pain is enough to ruin your day.

Yet, lying on his belly in the dirt, his face inches from the hole, our red-haired host was calling to the spider imploringly. "Come out!" Sam cried. "I want to meet you!" Imitating the scuttling of an insect—because bugs, not birds, are the Goliath's preferred prey—Sam wiggled a twig until he felt the spider grab it with the pedipalps, the food-handling feet at the front of the head. "She's pretty strong!" he commented. In the light of his headlamp, he could see the spider was female. Female tarantulas are bigger than males and in some species can live for thirty years. He wiggled the stick some more. A hissing sound issued from the burrow. Goliath birdeaters create this menacing sound by rubbing together pale bristles on the inside of the front legs. That did it. Sam gave us perhaps one second's notice before announcing, "Here she comes!"

The huge spider *thundered* out of the hole. Tipped with hooklike tarsi, each of her eight, seven-jointed legs thrummed loudly against the brittle leaf litter on the forest floor. Her head was the size of a small kiwi and her abdomen was as big as a clementine. This spider, Sam told us, wasn't even full grown, and perhaps two years old. Yet the youngster rushed fearlessly forward, shooting forward four or five inches as suddenly as a shiver—only to face three monsters who together weighed more than four thousand times as much as she did.

Finding no prey, the tarantula sensibly returned to the mouth of her tunnel, all her spider senses on alert. Her eight eyes were vestigial, but no matter. She could smell with her feet. She could taste with special hairs on her feet and legs.

And when she stood on the mat of silk she had spun from her own body at the mouth of her burrow, she could pick up the vibrations of the footfalls of the tiniest insect.

She knew we were there, Sam assured us. But she was unafraid.

It was as impressive as meeting a tiger. Yet I knew far more about tigers than spiders. I had of course seen plenty of spiders, but never really *met* one. This was about to change.

"Strike! Strike! Strike!" As Nic and I squatted beside him, Sam narrated the scene he was able watch with his flashlight, looking down another Goliath birdeater hole. The spider was attacking his stick. "Backing up . . . strike . . .

"She's not going to come out and play," Sam finally said with disappointment. "She's reared up and not very pleased with me." When threatened, tarantulas stand tall on their hind legs and raise their front ones like black belts ready to execute a karate chop. They display their long black fangs; sometimes a drop of venom exudes from one tip.

Sam didn't fear a bite—in twenty years of studying tarantulas, he'd never been bitten—but he withdrew his face from
the entrance of the hole. "She might start kicking hairs," he
explained. Rather than bite, an irritated Goliath birdeater is
apt to use the back legs to kick hairs off the abdomen, which,
floating on air currents, will lodge in an assailant's eyes, nose,
and skin, and cause pain and itching that can persist for hours.

This Sam didn't need, because, like us after our second
day surveying birdeater burrows, he was itchy enough from
the bites of other invertebrates, mainly ticks and chiggers.
Though Sam assured us this rainforest was "more benign than
the forest in Ohio," where he had his spider lab, we were all
consuming Benadryl and Exedrin each night to cope with the
itching, swelling, and sore muscles.

Nic and I were finding our days as exhausting as they were
exciting. "I ache all over," I wrote in my field journal on our
third day in French Guiana. "Drenched in sweat, covered with
dirt, and we've found so many ticks on our bodies we don't
even bother to look for them anymore." The birdeater dens
were usually found on slopes forty-five degrees or steeper, on
ground covered with giant slippery wet leaves and rotting logs

that gave way beneath our feet. Though there were only two common plants with skin-piercing spines—one a palm, the other a vine—we often encountered them, and in the 90-degree heat and 90 percent humidity, even small wounds could get seriously infected fast. Every brown leaf threatened to contain a stinging wasps' nest (Sam was stung on our second day), and in the litter and fallen trees, somewhere deadly fer-de-lance snakes were lurking.

So at the end of each day, it was a delight to retreat to Emerald Jungle Village, the nature center where we were staying. Run by the Dutch naturalist Joep Moonen and his wife, Marijke, it had whitewashed, tin-roofed guest quarters that featured fans, warm showers, and comfy mosquito-netted beds. Its extensive grounds were veined with paths through impressive gardens of native rainforest plants. Best of all, even amid such comfort, animals were all around us—even in our rooms. Gecko lizards slid like raindrops up and down exterior as well as interior walls. A toad inhabited our shower. One morning, before I got up, I watched from my bed as a small snake uncoiled and crawled across the floor from its hiding place in one of my shoes.

Naturally, Sam was eager to check every nook and cranny of our living quarters for possible tarantulas. He found one in the potted bromeliad on the tiled veranda just outside his room.

"Look! An *avicularia*!" Sam called to Nic and me one afternoon.

"Can I borrow your pen?" he asked me. He wasn't going to make a note. He inserted the pen between the succulent's serrated, pineapple-like leaves and gently prodded a tarantula the size of a child's fist to step forward—into his waiting hand.

"Sy," he said, "would you like to hold her?"

People aren't born with a fear of spiders—all sorts of psychological tests have proven that—but arachnophobia is an exceptionally easy fear to invoke. You can quickly teach a young person or animal to fear anything, including a harmless flower. But in experiments, people (and monkeys) will learn to fear a spider or snake much faster than they will learn to fear a plant. And like most Americans, I'd grown up hearing lots of bad spider PR. Several times in my youth and adulthood, when I'd woken up in the morning with a hot red bump somewhere, doctors had diagnosed the problem (usually incorrectly, insisted

Sam) as a spider bite—giving the false impression that spiders bite senselessly, without provocation, and, worse, that they're lurking everywhere, even in your bed. When I was growing up, my mother had warned me about black widow spiders, whose venom is reportedly fifteen times as toxic as a rattlesnake's. In Australia, I'd learned to be careful of the redback spider, a species closely related to black widows, which bites people far more often, as they particularly like dark places such as latrines, where they are sat upon. All of this was stored in my brain somewhere as Sam was offering to put a live wild tarantula into my hand.

I looked down to see that before I even answered, I had already stretched out my palm.

Sam nudged the back of her abdomen with my pen and she extended first one black hairy leg, then another, and another after another, until she was standing on my hand. The hooked tarsi at the tips of her feet felt vaguely prickly on my skin, like those of the Japanese beetles I have enjoyed holding since I was little. She stood for a moment while I admired her. She was a jet-haired beauty who looked like she had just had a fancy pedicure, the ends of her feet tipped in a bright, girly pink. For this reason, her species is known as the pinktoe tarantula. They're exceptionally docile and seldom bite. Even their hairs are not usually irritating.

She began to walk. Slowly at first, stepping forward with her front legs, she crossed my right palm into my waiting left, just as my first dime-store turtle, Ms. Yellow Eyes, would do when I was a child. The tarantula probably weighed about as much as my turtle had.

And then something magical happened. Holding her in my hand, I could literally feel a connection with this creature. No longer did I see her as a really big spider; now I saw her as a small animal. Of course she was both. "Animals" include not only mammals but also birds and reptiles, amphibians and insects, fish and spiders, and many more. But perhaps because the tarantula was furry, like a chipmunk, and big enough to handle, now I saw her and her spider kin in a new light. She was a unique individual, and in my hand, she was in my care. A wave of tenderness swept over me as I watched her walk, softly, slowly, and deliberately, across my skin.

Until, that is, she started to speed up. What was she doing?

"They do speed up, and sometimes they bunch up and launch," said Sam. When this happens in his lab, he advises students to step away, unless they want a flying tarantula land-ing on them. Though pinktoes build their silky retreats in the eaves of buildings, in shrubs, and in the curves of leaves on pineapple plantations, they know they belong in trees, and if they feel threatened, they usually head upward.

Now I was nervous—so nervous, in fact, that I began to shake. But my concern was not that a tarantula might run up my face. I felt faint with fear that if she launched, this beautiful, gentle animal might land on the tiled veranda and hurt herself. Since like all spiders she wore her skeleton on the outside, it was possible that a fall could break her exoskeleton. A beautiful wild creature might lose her life. And it would be my fault.

"I think I'd better put her back," I told Sam. I returned her to his hand and he replaced her on the bromeliad, where she retreated to her silken home.

✧

THAT EVENING WHEN WE RETURNED FROM THE DAY'S DEN census, she was still there. "I think we have a pet tarantula," Sam announced. He named her Clarabelle.

It was a fitting name for a pretty and elegant lady—which

Clarabelle was. Tarantulas, Sam explained to us, are "tidy little homemakers," lining their hideaways, whether in trees or in the ground, with fresh, dry silk. "They're like regular Martha Stewarts!" Sam told us. Despite spiders' reputations as dirty, nasty "bugs," tarantulas are as immaculate as cats, carefully cleaning any dirt that falls on their bodies by meticulously drawing the hairs on their legs through the mouth, using their fangs like the teeth of a comb.

We grew increasingly fond of Clarabelle. Mornings and evenings, we'd check on her to make sure she was okay. Tarantulas are well armed against their enemies, but some do succumb. Occasionally, an agile-fingered mammal— a particularly stoic monkey or an exceptionally tough coatimundi— will withstand the shower of irritating hairs to fish a tarantula from her hole and eat her. So will certain birds. Female pepsis wasps, hummingbird-size flying insects, sting tarantulas into paralysis; then they lay eggs in their flesh so that when they hatch, the larvae can feast on the living spider. I sometimes worried about Clarabelle during the day, and was always relieved when we'd return to find her safe in her bromeliad.

I wondered: Did Clarabelle know us? "Spiders are individuals like everyone else," Sam assured us. He's had pet tarantulas since he was thirteen, and in his lab in Ohio, he had about five hundred of them. Through the years of interacting with them, Sam learned that within the same species, some individuals seemed calm and others nervous. Some changed their behavior over time and appeared to grow calmer in his presence. Later, with Nic, I'd visit his tarantula lab. One of his students noted that something unusual happened when Sam walked in. Even though many of his tarantulas were natural-ly blind, when Sam—and only Sam—entered the room, five hundred tarantulas invariably turned in their terrariums and oriented toward him.

AS THE DAYS PASSED, IT SEEMED THAT CLARABELLE WAS growing calmer as we handled her. This could have been, of course, that we were growing more used to her. Perhaps she was inadvertently teaching us to be calm and responding to our increasing ease in holding a spider. All three of us enjoyed interacting so intimately with this small wild ani-mal. She made us feel even more at home at Emerald Jungle Village.

One day Nic tossed her a katydid and took her portrait as she was eating it. Most spiders, after injecting prey with paralyzing venom, pump fluid from their stomach into the victim to liquefy the meal, then suck it dry and toss the skin away. Tarantulas do it differently. Clarabelle ground up her food with teeth behind her fangs. Though I felt bad for the katydid—a relative of the friendly, familiar cricket—I loved that we could give something to Clarabelle. For she herself had much to give, and was about to become a spider ambassador.

✧

THE MORNING OF OUR LAST FULL DAY IN FRENCH GUIANA, Sam urged Clarabelle into a plastic deli carton. We were taking her with us on our last trip to Trésor Réserve, after which she would be released back at the potted plant where she was found. But first Sam had organized a meeting for her with some people who, like her, were small but important.

By the head of the trail leading into the jungle, they were waiting: nine children from the local school, ages six through ten, had come from the nearby village of Roura. Joep introduced them to Sam in French. *"On voit aujourd'hui*

Dr. Marshall . . ." But Sam was eager to introduce the real guest of honor. Removing the deli carton from his backpack, he carefully peeled off the lid. One hairy leg arched over the lip of the container, and then another and another, until Clarabelle stepped calmly onto Sam's palm.

"*Qui veux la toucher?*" he asked the children.

Who wants to touch her?

For a moment, nobody spoke. One little girl had earlier confessed she was afraid of spiders. But then a ten-year-old boy in a baseball cap raised his hand. Sam showed him how to extend his palm to let Clarabelle step aboard. She moved so delicately and deliberately that soon nine little palms stretched out to hold her—even the little girl who said she was afraid.

Nic took many photos for our book that day. I still love to look at the hands of those kids: brown hands, pink hands, gently cupped to welcome the footfall of a creature that some of them had only moments earlier viscerally feared. In one photo, three girls huddle together to let Clarabelle stroll across their skin. Their eyes look down on the spider with concentration and reverence; their faces are relaxed with the sense of peace and wholeness that only holding a small, charming animal can bring. Now they saw a wild creature in their native forests in an entirely new way. That day, I heard a little girl in neat pigtails murmur, almost under her breath, *"Elle est belle, le monstre."* She is beautiful, the monster.

✧

By allowing me to handle her, Clarabelle had opened to me a spidery world I'd previously never appreciated. Her great size was only the most obvious aspect of her magnificence. Like all spiders, she possessed astonishing superpowers. Since she wore her skeleton on the outside, she could shed her outer covering—and even the lining of her mouth, stomach, and lungs—when she needed to grow. If a leg was injured, she could pull it off, eat it, and grow a new one. From her own body she could pull silk, and by this action transform what began as a liquid to a solid softer than cotton but stronger than steel.

Creatures with these same gifts were so common at home that I had passed them without notice. In our basement in Hancock, we had cellar spiders with elongated bodies and elegant legs, who hung upside down and vibrated their webs disconcertingly if you touched them. In the woodpile, we often found jumping spiders, who had excellent vision and seemed to notice us and leap aside. We had many spiders living in the barn, and when one would inevitably weave a web by Christopher's pen, naturally it reminded me of a scene from *Charlotte's Web*. Of course, I would never have hurt a spider. In our farmhouse, I didn't vacuum enough to endanger their webs. If a spider appeared in a bothersome spot—in the tub, or on my pillow, for instance—Howard or I would carefully capture the creature in a yogurt cup and transport it outside.

But perhaps because they were so small, perhaps because they were so common, or perhaps because they were invertebrates, with lives so unlike the birds, mammals, and reptiles I knew so much better, I'd never before given spiders much thought.

Now, thanks to Clarabelle, even the most ordinary corners of our home were freshly enchanted. The world, I realized, brimmed even fuller with life than I had suspected, rich with the souls of tiny creatures who may love their lives as much as we love ours.

⚹ CHAPTER 5 ⚹
THE CHRISTMAS WEASEL

*I*T WAS CHRISTMAS MORNING, AND TIME FOR THE traditional feast for our flock of hens. As Tess chewed her celebratory rawhide in the house and Christopher slurped his hot mash in his pen, I brought the Ladies a big bowl of hot, fresh popcorn to start the holiday, as I always did. But on this morning, I was greeted with a sad surprise. One of my Ladies, a beloved older black-and-white hen of the heritage Dominique breed, was dead on the floor, her head wedged into a hole in the corner of the coop.

I stooped to lift the fallen chicken up by her scaly yellow legs. But I couldn't. Something—or some*one*—had ahold of her head and wouldn't let go. I pulled and pulled. Finally, her body came free. An instant later, out from the hole popped a white head smaller than a walnut, with coal-black eyes, a pink nose . . . and flecks of crimson blood on the white fur around its mouth. It was an ermine, a tiny weasel in its winter-white color phase. It stared directly into my eyes.

I had never seen one before. It was gorgeous. The ermine's fur was the purest white I had ever seen, whiter than snow or cloud or sea foam—so white it seemed to glow, like the garment of an angel. No wonder kings trimmed their robes in ermine fur. But even more impressive was its gaze—a look so bold and fearless that it knocked the breath from my lungs. Here was a creature the length of my hand, who weighed little more than a handful of change, but who had come out of its hole expressly to challenge me even as I towered menacingly above. *What are you doing with my chicken?* those coal eyes said to me. *Give it back!*

Of course, I had been thinking it was *my* chicken. Like my friend had done with the first flock of hens she gave me, I had hand-raised this hen, as I had all of her sisters, from a fluffy chick still egg-shaped two days after hatching. Our chicks grow up in my home office, cheerfully perching on my lap and shoulders as I write, or racing around the floor after one another, spreading wood shavings and feather dust. They occasionally add to my prose by walking across my computer keyboard.

As a result of their upbringing, everyone in the flock was remarkably affectionate. After I had moved their headquarters from my office to their coop in the barn and they began their free-range careers in the yard, they would rush to mob Howard and me whenever we stepped outside. They made us feel like rock stars. Then they'd squat in front of us to be stroked or picked up and kissed on their combs. They'd hang out with Christopher Hogwood when he was out on his tether, sometimes stealing scraps. They were unperturbed by Tess, who was too focused on the Frisbee to chase them. They followed Howard and me as we did yard work, commenting constantly in their lilting chicken voices: *Here I am. Where are you? Any worms? Oh, a bug! Over here* . . . At night when I closed them into their coop, they'd fly up to their perches—each has a regular position, next to her best friends—and I'd stroke them and let their contented nighttime clucks and trills sweep over me like a lullaby.

The dead hen was one of the Ladies who'd been with us longest. She had helped to teach the younger chicks the parameters of our joint property with Kate, Jane, and Lila, warned the babies about crossing the street, called to them when she spotted a hawk. She was one who came most eagerly to be petted and fed, and had even taken to perching on the folding chairs beside the table we set outside beneath the big silver maple, where we'd eat in summer.

Her body was still warm as I held her in my hands. Before me was her killer. You'd think I'd have been overwhelmed with anger, out for vengeance. It had happened before. My first day of kindergarten, I saw a little boy pulling the legs off a daddy longlegs. I bit him, and to my parents' horror, I was sent home in ignominy. In college, I'd had another incident. Furious when I'd learned that a former boyfriend's roommate had lied about him to authorities, I set out to confront him. But I unexpectedly ran into the guy on my way up the stairs to find him. To our mutual surprise—I'm small with bird-like bones—I grabbed the man by his collar and threw him against the wall. I was shaking with rage and shocked at the strength it gave me.

As a young adult, I feared anger, because I thought it was in my blood. Though my father was so respected that I heard a subordinate once fainted with fear before him, he was even-tempered. But my mother was capable of dizzying wrath. When I was in high school, I'd invited a boyfriend to join me at a Saturday-night Bible study a few blocks from our house. He'd told his parents to pick him up at our house afterward. My parents were out that night—and though we never went inside our house, when my parents came home first, my mother, who had been drinking, shrieked at us with rage. I had been strictly told not to let any boy in the house when my parents weren't home. I hadn't. Nonetheless, my mother threatened to take me to the hospital to determine whether I had lost my virginity. Somehow my father dissuaded her from this errand, but I was banned from seeing the boy, and from attending Bible study, for a long time afterward. (Many years later, I realized why my mother was so angry. With the aid of several martinis, she worried that a neighbor might have seen a boy standing outside the empty house with her daughter and concluded we were the "wrong kind" of family.)

Anger haunted my mother as my father lay dying from cancer. One afternoon while we were on opposite sides of my father's bed, at the mention of some ordinary financial detail, my mother clenched her slender, manicured hand into a claw and took a swipe at my face. I caught her delicate wrist in midair. She had swung at me so hard that my hand, stopping hers, left a bruise on her skin. My father made me apologize to her.

THE
ERMINE'S FUR

WAS THE PUREST WHITE
I HAD EVER SEEN,
WHITER THAN SNOW OR
CLOUD OR SEA FOAM—

SO WHITE
IT SEEMED TO
GLOW, LIKE
THE GARMENT OF
AN ANGEL.

But toward the ermine, who had killed someone I loved, I felt no anger at all.

Here before me was one of the world's smallest carnivores. It is as if all the ferocity of the world's wild hunters—lions, tigers, wolverines—has been concentrated into a creature who weighs less than half a pound. Quick as lightning, an ermine can leap into the air to kill a bird as it takes flight, or follow a lemming down a tunnel. It can swim, climb trees, and bring down an animal many times its size with a single bite to the neck—and then drag it away. An ermine consumes five to ten meals a day. It needs to eat at least a quarter to a third of its own weight just to survive in captivity, and much more in the wild, especially during the cold winter. These little animals' hearts beat nearly four hundred times a minute. No wonder they kill everything they can at every opportunity. They are glorious in their single-minded ferocity.

I then understood something important about my mother. She was, in her way, as fierce as that ermine. She was the only child of a postmaster and an ice man in a tiny town in Arkansas. She grew up with three strikes against her: she was poor, she lived in a rural area, and she was a female. Yet at a time when girls were discouraged from education and adventure, she had learned to fly a plane, had gone to college, made valedictorian of her class, landed a job at the FBI, and married an army officer. She'd grown up in a house where she could see chickens scratching in the dirt beneath the floorboards of the kitchen. Sometimes she had hunted squirrels to eat; her old shotgun still rested in the corner of a bedroom closet in each house where my family had lived. But through the force of her will and her intellect, she had transformed it all: the military gave her servants to clean the house, mow the lawn; a chef cooked at her parties. Her husband had a staff car, a yacht, and a plane at his disposal. As a child, I had always looked to my father, a survivor of the Bataan Death March and a decorated war hero, as my model of courage and persistence, but my mother's example, too, had helped me to grow up believing that if anything could be done by a human, it could be done by me. Her achievement was a feat as staggering as an ermine taking down a hen.

My mother had died of pancreatic cancer earlier that year. In the hospital in Virginia, I held her hand as she fearlessly breathed her last. Since the doctors at Fort Belvoir had diagnosed her with this painful terminal disease, she had not once whined or wept. As I looked into the piercing black eyes of that white weasel, I realized how much I had admired my mother, and how much I missed her.

✧

THE ERMINE HELD MY GAZE FOR PERHAPS THIRTY SECONDS. Then it popped back into the hole. I desperately wanted to run to the house to get Howard so he could see it. What were the chances the tiny animal would still be there, much less show itself again, when I came back? I put down the hen where I had found her, ran the hundred feet to the house, and alerted Howard. Together we returned to the coop. Again I picked up the hen. And again the ermine shot its head from the hole, its black eyes blazing from that luminous white face as its laser stare fearlessly met ours.

Even in the wake of tragedy, we could not have felt more amazed had we been visited by an angel that Christmas morning. When the angel met the shepherds in Bethlehem, the shepherds "were sore afraid." When I was a child, that phrase had always seemed odd to me. In my illustrated Bible, the angels looked like pretty ladies in nightgowns with wings, and on our Christmas tree, they were always playing harps or blowing trumpets. Though the flying was impressive, nothing about those angels would have scared me, even as a little girl. But now that I have thought more deeply about these words of scripture, it seems to me that the angels must have been more like our Christmas weasel: glorious in purity, strength, and holy perfection.

In our barn we beheld a great wonder, as did the shepherds who flocked to a different barn so long ago. Our Christmas blessing came down not from heaven but up from a burrow in the earth. With dazzlingly white fur, a hammering pulse, and a bottomless appetite, the ermine was ablaze with life. Like a struck match chases away darkness, this creature's incandescent presence left no room for anger in my heart—for it had been stretched wide with awe, and flooded with the balm of forgiveness.

CHAPTER 6
TESS

FOR MOST OF OUR LIVES TOGETHER, TESS INTERRUPT-ed our work constantly to lay joy in our laps.

After our morning outing, when we'd feed Christopher and the Ladies, Tess would sit quietly in my office or in Howard's for about an hour. Then she'd have had enough. As we were writing, suddenly a ball or a Frisbee would appear on one of our laps. We'd have to go outside together to play.

There were times—in the middle of writing a crucial transition, for instance, or during the birth of a new idea—that the intrusion of a toy, wet with a dog's drool, was unwelcome. But not for long. For many reasons, nothing could be more fun, more life-affirming, or more meaningful, than playing with our joyous, athletic border collie.

Playing with Tess meant multitasking love. Whenever Tess went out, the person with her always interacted with the other

SHE WAS NOT ONLY POWERFUL, BUT REFINED AND ELEGANT—THE VERY DEFINITION OF GRACE.

animals too. Christopher would sense our presence and call, "Unh. Unh! UNH!" He demanded that we pet him, feed him a scoop of grain, an apple, or some slops, or let him out to be hooked up on his tether. The Ladies would mob us, squatting to be petted, picked up, and kissed.

Happily, if we worked quickly, there was time to do all this between tosses, because Tess liked you to throw the ball or fling the Frisbee a L-O-N-G way. Howard could send the disk flying hundreds of feet. I couldn't. Plus I had bad aim. But still, Tess caught anything that was tossed without fail, no matter who threw it. Howard called her "a real Golden Glover." She never played favorites. If we were out together, or with visitors, she would always alternate between people, handing the toy back to first one person, then the next. She loved the game so much, I think, that she assumed we must too, so she kept track out of a sense of fairness. Nobody should be left out. If she had summoned Howard to play earlier, while we were working, she would pick me an hour later.

The sight of our spirited young dog racing over our field, leaping up to catch the toy, always lifted me, like singing the first notes of "Amazing Grace." Her movements matched the song's first words, too. She was not only powerful, but refined and elegant—the very definition of grace. And particularly considering the injuries Tess had sustained from the terrible snowplow accident, and before that, the sorrow of her early life as an unwanted puppy, her grace and her happiness with us was nothing short of amazing.

The joy Tess brought continued into the night. The last thing we'd do before going to bed was play one more round of Frisbee. Her black-and-white form was gorgeous gilded in moonlight. But I think Tess was even more beautiful on inky black moonless nights, when I couldn't see her at all.

On our country road, no streetlights pollute the night skies. Some nights are almost cave dark, and we humans can see nothing on these moonless nights. But Tess could see perfectly in the dark.

Dogs possess a *tapedum lucedum*, a light-gathering reflector in the eye—the reason dogs' and cats' eyes glow in the headlights of a car. So, on those darkest of nights, I would follow her into the blackness, listening for the jingle of her dog tags. She would lead me down the gentle slope of the backyard to where the lawn leveled out at the edge of the field. Then I would whisper to her. "Tess . . . Go!"

I'd wait some seconds and then toss the Frisbee into the

blackness. Where it went, I had no idea. But a second or two later, I'd hear the beautiful click of her teeth on the plastic—and know that she had leapt into the air and caught it.

I'd squat down and hold my hands out in the dark. She always put the Frisbee directly in my outstretched palms—Tess knew that otherwise I'd have to waste valuable play time feeling about for it on the ground.

Tess had quickly learned to intuit almost our every move. She always knew when we were going to the upper barn versus the lower barn, when we were going to get in the car versus go in the house. Inside the house, it seemed she even knew what room we'd be heading for before we did. When we'd take long hikes together—sometimes Howard and I would take a day off and bring her with us to hike in the White Mountains—she'd run ahead to catch up with my long-legged husband, then run back to me. Often she'd know to find me just before a fork in the trail—where, without her, I'd inevitably have chosen the wrong direction. Then she'd run ahead to Howard, and then back to check on me. Howard noted she'd hiked the same trail as he and I did, but did it four or five times before the humans reached the end. Bred for synching sheep with shepherd, border collies are celebrated for their brilliant minds. Tess applied hers to figuring out what we might do next together, and how she might best be of help.

Even in her brilliance, Tess couldn't possibly have understood my blindness in the dark. How could I not see what was so clear to her? Yet she generously worked around my unfathomable disability. She always patiently brought the toy right to my hands. And when I felt we should go in, I only had to say softly, "Tess, come." She would run back to me and then lead me by the sound of her jingling tags back to the house.

Though Tess constantly amazed me with her intelligence, strength, and agility, I think I most clearly saw how richly she blessed me on those dark nights. For unlike most other humans, thanks to Tess, I could voyage, even play, in the pitch blackness. When I was with her, she loaned me her dog superpowers—powers I did not myself possess but had longed for ever since I had first seen them in Molly.

But eventually, that would change, and change me profoundly.

✦

ON A JUNE MORNING, JUST AS WE WERE WAKING UP, TESS jumped down from the bed, stood up, and fell over.

At first I thought it was arthritis. Tess was then fourteen, and between her age and the snowplow injury she'd sustained before we'd met her, it was no wonder that she stumbled sometimes. Our marvelous vet, Chuck DeVinne, was already treating Christopher, then twelve, for age-related joint ailments, and every morning I hid capsules containing three medicines in a breakfast muffin.

But when I looked into Tess's eyes, it was clear this was not morning stiffness. She was having a mini-stroke.

She seemed to recover quickly and completely. But her brush with disaster put us on notice. Though Howard and I were in our forties, the animals with whom we'd shared our vibrant youth were rushing ahead of us into old age. Our days together were numbered.

Of course, they always had been. To me, one of the most heartbreaking conditions of life on Earth is that most of the animals we love, with the exception of some parrots and tortoises, die so long before we do. I used to joke with friends as I left for trips to lands with poisonous snakes, man-eating carnivores, and active landmines that I was trying to make sure I predeceased Chris and Tess. I never feared dying. Death was just one more new place to go. We'd all go there eventually. I believed if there was a heaven, and if I went there, I would be reunited with all the animals I had loved. But I deeply dreaded being left behind when Chris and Tess passed on.

Still, as I constantly reminded myself, they both seemed to be doing just fine as seniors. Chris's appreciation for the best things in life—gentle touch, loving company, and chocolate donuts—continued unabated. He still amassed new fans for Pig Spa. Tess charmed everyone, as before, as she leapt to catch the Frisbee, and ran after the ball till *we* stopped her, when her tongue was hanging out.

Then one day, distracted by an interesting smell, Tess dropped her Frisbee in the grass. When Howard asked her to pick it up, she ignored him. She had gone deaf. It had probably happened weeks or months before, and because her sensitivity and intellect had so effectively compensated, we hadn't even noticed.

Then came a bout with canine peripheral vestibular disease. The symptoms are like those of a stroke, but to the sufferer they feel very different. Tess's world spun uncontrollably. Beset with vertigo and nausea, she couldn't stand up for weeks.

Incredibly, she emerged from this, too, like the fighter she was. She would enjoy walks again, but with a decided head tilt forever after. And by now her bright brown eyes had grown cloudy. Deaf and going blind, she could no longer play Frisbee. The ball held no interest. My heart ached—and at first, I thought it ached for her. Surely, I thought, she must miss our hikes, our hours of play, racing across the field to catch the ball and the Frisbee.

I was wrong. The heartache was my own. I was the one who longed for those younger, stronger days, for the magic of her more-than-human gifts of hearing frequencies I could not detect, seeing with surety in the dark. I missed traveling in the slipstream of her superpowers. I was sad—but Tess was not.

One look at her showed she was happy. Her tail wagged. Her smile, her ears, her composure, all radiated contentment. Tess didn't feel like chasing or leaping. Life was still rich and interesting, redolent with scent, and full of tasty treats and the comfort of being with those she loved. She accepted that now, for some reason, the world had gone largely dark and quiet. But she wasn't worried. Clearly, she understood that somehow we humans could navigate this black and soundless world for her.

Tess still enjoyed going outside, even at night. I used to love how she could run so far away from me to catch the toy; now I rejoiced that we stayed so close together. Tess could follow my heat and my scent at first. Later, we remained touching at all times. And I was honored, after our years together, to receive the gift of her graceful, trusting reliance on me, as I had once relied on her, to navigate through the dark. Never before had anyone relied on me so completely. Never before had anyone loved me more deeply. And never before had I experienced grace so profound.

In her wobbly old age, Tess still made me want to sing. Her grace was now even more amazing. Hers was the grace to which we appeal when we need strength or compassion of greater-than-human origin. Grace is not merely athletic prowess or elegance of movement. It is also, theologians tell us, the divine ability to regenerate and sanctify, inspire and strengthen: "I once was lost but now am found / was blind but now I see."

Tess never lost her superpowers. She had simply brought them back and handed them to me, like the Frisbee at night. Until the end of our days together, I would enjoy the humbling privilege of doing for her what she had done for me. Now it was I who would lead *her* through the darkness.

My love for my dog and my pig burned ever brighter as they aged. There was no darkness we couldn't navigate together. But what about when Chris and Tess were gone?

CHAPTER 7
CHRIS AND TESS II

AFTER CHRIS AND, TOO SOON AFTERWARD, TESS had died, the one thing that kept me going was the comforting thought that I could kill myself.

Tess, sixteen, was already failing when we found that Christopher had died in his sleep in his pen on a morning in early summer. I was in shock. We had no warning. At age fourteen, Chris had a bit of arthritis but otherwise seemed fine. Because he had shown no symptoms of rapid decline, and because we had no idea how long pigs could live, I had hoped he would outlive Tess and help me through her death. But this was not to be.

In her final days, Tess had endured my flushing her body daily with infusions of Ringer's solution to aid her failing kidneys. At night, sometimes she woke whimpering, with confusion or nightmares—I never knew which. I knew it was only a matter of time before her life held more pain than pleasure. That time came one short season later, on a sunny September afternoon, when our vet came to our home, and, as Howard and I held Tess in our arms beneath our silver maple, gave her the shot that ended her brilliant, big-hearted life.

How I wanted to go with her! Losing Christopher was horrendous enough. Without Chris, the barn, even with our busy hens, felt empty. Just looking at our yard made me sick with grief. After his loss, I had lived for Tess. I knew she was dying, and I think she did too. But we were together, and for those short months, for both of us, that was enough.

Once she was gone, though I still had my darling hens, my beloved husband, our lovely home, friends who cared, and meaningful work—blessings that had brought joy to every day—it all felt like nothing. It was early autumn, my favorite time of year, and the air smelled like ripening apples. But I didn't want the precious fruit of our hundred-year-old Roxbury russets. I didn't want to pick the last of summer's blueberries. I didn't look forward to the fall colors or the fluffy snow. I didn't want food or sleep, music or company. I didn't want Christmas, or Easter, or next year—or ever. I hated myself for my ingratitude.

Weeks went by, and then months. Still my despair felt bottomless. My hair fell out. My gums bled. Worse, there was something wrong with my brain. When I spoke with people, I would search for a word in my mind but speak its opposite. Once I was at an elderly friend's house and tried to make a little joke about an eighty-year-old acquaintance who was dating a sixty-year-old. I wanted to say he was "robbing the cradle." But to my horror it came out "He's robbing the grave"!

I knew I was dangerously depressed. Alarmed, I fought to quell it. I forced myself to swallow food and water. I took vitamins. As before, I worked out three times a week at the health club. I spent time outside every day to get sunshine. Attempting to revive my ailing brain, I got tapes to play in my car to learn Italian. Nothing helped.

And for the first time in decades, I could not escape into my work. After Christopher died, to honor him, I'd begun writing a memoir of our life together. So every day, my work was to recount, in vivid detail, the fourteen years of comfort and joy that Christopher, and Tess, and the friends who had gathered around them to become family, had brought to me—comfort and joy now forever lost. Even the little girls next door had moved away. Writing the book was not cathartic. It was draining and difficult.

I struggled every day to finish the manuscript. And what then? Chris and Tess would still be dead. Would I still feel like this for the rest of my life?

I thought: *I can't stand this.*

And I remembered the injectable Valium left over from my mother's failed battle with cancer. After her death, I had taken it home with me, meaning to dispose of it safely. But I never had.

I MADE MYSELF A DEAL. IF I DIDN'T FEEL ANY BETTER BY THE time the manuscript was finished, I would end my pain, as vets end many animals', with a simple injection. I'd overdose on Valium. I didn't know then that this plan wouldn't work. An overdose of injected Valium wouldn't kill me; it would only make me sleep longer than usual. And because of the nature of depression, I also didn't realize what a hideous blow my suicide would deal my survivors. Killing myself would only deflect my pain onto those I loved—the last thing in the world I'd have intended.

But the decision brought me a strange sense of peace. Knowing I would not have to suffer like this forever, I could soldier on until I had fulfilled my obligations. There was at least an end in sight. Either I would feel better and go on with my life, or I wouldn't, and could end it.

Besides the Hogwood manuscript, I had one more duty to discharge before I could make the decision. I'd signed a contract for a shorter book, for younger readers, about the work of Dr. Lisa Dabek, an extraordinary researcher who had just begun radio tracking a species of kangaroo that lives in trees in Papua New Guinea. Lisa had become a good friend since I'd first met her at a talk on my Amazon pink dolphin book years before, and I owed her the honor of featuring her important work in this book. The expedition to her study site was slated for March—a particularly depressing time in New Hampshire, when the snow is melting into mud and everything looks gray and dirty. It might be, I thought, the last expedition of my life.

✧

THE FIRST THREE HOURS OF THE HIKE TO OUR FIELD SITE would be the hardest, Lisa promised. Certainly, it *had* to get easier from here, I thought. With each step up the muddy, sometimes forty-five-degree slope through the cloud forest, my heart banged in my chest like a bongo drummer gone berserk. Holding on to my walking stick, I gasped for breath. An eight-year-old from the village was carrying my backpack because I could not. One of the local women who was working as a porter extended a scabby hand to help me. She clearly had a skin disease. I grabbed her hand gratefully. Sweat, sore muscles, contagious skin ailments—none of it mattered. Neither did the painful swipe of stinging nettles, or the leeches that brush off from the tips of leaves and can end up in your eye. All that mattered was putting one foot in front of the other until the first three hours were over and we could sit down and take a break.

Then there would be only six more hours of hiking to go—that day.

Lisa's field site, in the 10,000-foot-tall mountains of Papua New Guinea's Huon Peninsula, was so remote that to her knowledge, no white people other than those on her research teams had ever seen it. It would take us—eight researchers, plus forty-four men, women, and children from the village of Yawan carrying our camping and scientific gear and food—three days of strenuous hiking to reach it.

Exhausted, I sat down with the others on top of a ridge. It was here, Lisa told me encouragingly, that a member of a previous team, a thirty-year-old bodybuilder, threw up and confessed he thought he could go no farther. (He made it, though.) At last I could look at more than my feet slipping on the muddy ground. I raised my eyes to unspeakable beauty. Far below us, in the distance, were the tidy villages of Yawan and Towet, with their grass roofs and neat gardens of vegetables and flowers. Around us, massive trees hung heavy with moss like velvet drapes; wild rhododendrons and ginger punctuated the green with their red and orange flowers. Tree ferns' orange fiddleheads swelled larger than cabbages, recalling the dawn of the world. The air twinkled with the chatter of parakeets. Two members of our team—one a veterinarian from Seattle, the other a zookeeper from Minneapolis—started singing. Our Papuan friends joined in. Everyone seemed to be having a good time. I was focused entirely on finishing the hike. If I had dropped dead, it would have been fine with me, but I didn't want to wreck the expedition for everyone else.

✧

SIX HOURS LATER, AS EVERYONE WAS HURRYING TO PITCH tents in the rain, I wandered off into the trackless cloud forest to throw up.

This wasn't a very good idea. A person can disappear in the cloud forest in seconds. The rain was pouring down hard enough to wash away my tracks and drown out calling voices. But I wasn't calling for help. I didn't realize it, but I had both altitude sickness and hypothermia and had taken leave of my senses. My lips and fingertips were blue when my friend Nic, the book's photographer, found me and led me, still dazed, back to a tent.

Quickly Lisa and the vet stripped off my soaked clothes, swaddled me in a sleeping bag, and brought me a hot drink. "Is there anything else you want?" Lisa asked kindly.

By now my mind had started functioning again. "Yes," I said, "if someone can find my backpack . . ." What I wanted was in my zippered toiletry kit. Along with my silver wedding ring, I had stored another treasure there, so they wouldn't slip off during the hike. It was a hollow silver bracelet a friend had given me after Tess died. It contained some of Tess's ashes.

✧

THE NEXT MORNING, AFTER ANOTHER GRUELING THREE-hour hike, we set up camp at the place called Wasaunon, our home base for the next two weeks as the team sought to find, radio-collar, release, and track the endangered Matschie's tree kangaroos. Lisa's work was essential: discovering the 'roos' range and their needs would yield a blueprint for protecting the cloud forest.

At our campsite, ancient tall trees stood guard over our tents like benign wizards bearded in moss. The moss was studded with ferns. The ferns were dotted with lichens and liverworts, fungi and orchids. But it was the moss that most enchanted me. The world seemed cloaked in its velvet, as if the clouds in these tall mountains had congealed into green and come alive. John Ruskin, a nineteenth-century British art critic, called moss—humble, soft, and ancient—"the first mercy of the Earth." Mercy, then, was everywhere around me: it covered tree trunks, vines, the ground, forgiving every clumsy step and cushioning every fall.

Moss hung in great orange clumps from the branches. It was exactly the color of the tree kangaroos. "For years, that's all we saw," Lisa told me. And those elusive tree kangaroos were surely up there sitting on those soft cushions of moss

right now. The Matschie's tree kangaroo, the species Lisa studies, is about the size of a big cat. With mostly brownish-orange
fur (except on the belly, which is lemon yellow), it has a moist
pink nose, and a long furry tail. Dr. Seuss could not have
come up with a creature more adorable, nor Gund a plushie
that you'd more want to hug. Our job, among the ferns and
the orchids, the mist and the moss, was to find, radio-collar,
and then follow animals that looked like they belonged in a
children's storybook.

✧

"AT ABOUT 11, A MIRACLE," I WROTE IN MY FIELD DIARY.
"The trackers came back bearing a long-beaked echidna! Native only to New Guinea, it is another Seuss character come
to life—a fat, furry, pillow of a body with only a few spines,
dear, tiny black eyes, back feet that seem to be on backwards
and a six-inch tubular snout that is so long he literally trips on
it as he trundles along."

Our guest seemed remarkably unperturbed at his capture,
and immediately upon his release from the tracker's coffee
bag began to explore, using his strong hands to tear a hole

through the lashed-together saplings we were using as a table. He stabbed his nose into the earth as if it were water, and then walked though the sapling wall of our makeshift cookhouse as easily as smoke. He did not recoil when I gently touched his back, finding his charcoal-colored fur surprisingly soft— though his few ivory spines were quite sharp. Perhaps that is what gave him confidence. Still, we didn't want to stress him. Though we could have watched him forever, rapt, after photographing and videotaping him for ten minutes, we returned him to his coffee bag and took him back home.

"It seems only minutes have elapsed since his visit when another team of trackers brings us a mountain cuscus!" continues my field diary. "He is a plump, plush fellow, with huge brown eyes, his woolly fur dark brown except for his moon-white belly, pink hands, feet, and underside of his naked, grasping tail."

At every turn, it seemed, we encountered evidence of rare, unlikely animals with incredible bodies, fantastic abilities, and delightful names. Echidnas are egg-laying mammals, one of only two kinds on Earth (the platypus is the other). Mountain cuscus are the largest possums in the world, weighing up to thirteen pounds, nocturnal and secretive. Other animals we didn't actually see, but we found their nests, hides, and holes. We encountered a mound where a chicken-size brush fowl had dug a nest as big as a Volkswagen in the dirt, using the heat generated by compost to incubate his eggs. (Yes, the male tends them, adjusting the temperature as needed, cooling by digging ventilation holes.) We found holes in the grassy areas near camp that had been dug by pademelons—fat, furry kangaroo-like characters with alert, swiveling ears and stubby tails. The trackers reported they spotted a dorcopsis, a tiny wallaby with the face of a gazelle, near camp.

This cloud forest world was vividly alive in a way I had not observed in any other habitat. Unlike in the Amazon and other rainforests I had visited, there were no mosquitoes (too cold), no biting ants, no poisonous snakes, spiders, or scorpions. Though Wasaunon was teeming with lives, all of them seemed not only benign but benevolent.

Each day revealed a new, delightful surprise: Wild strawberries along a path. Micro-orchids smaller than a dress-maker's pin. Nights shot through with falling stars. The humans around me were wonderful too: from the United States, New Zealand, Australia, and Papua New Guinea. Three of us were friends before the trip; by the end of the first week, we all were.

Trackers and scientists, natives and foreigners, whether zoo-keeper, artist, or researcher, we were united in the challenging task of exploring this primeval cloud forest in the effort to protect it.

Life in camp was not always easy. The tree 'roos were elu-sive. Our clothes were always wet. Nights and mornings, we could see our breath. Curled as tight as a fist in my sleeping bag, I slept in all my clothes but still woke up cold every day. But the work was essential, the camaraderie warm, and the setting magical.

Early one morning, we felt the ground tremble. It was an earthquake, which here would do us no harm. In fact, the tremors felt reassuring to me. "The Earth feels so new here," I wrote in my field journal. "No wonder we can sometimes feel its molten, beating heart."

✧

FROM THE MOMENT SHE WOKE ON APRIL 1, LISA TOLD ME, she felt it would be a good day. We both liked to get up early to see the trackers leave on their search for tree kangaroos. I was deeply impressed by the men's kindness, not only toward the Westerners (whose heads New Guinea tribes had once famously hunted) but also toward the animals, whose skins adorned their ceremonial clothes and whose flesh they used to eat less than a generation ago.

Lisa was washing clothes and I was doing the dinner dishes down by the stream when we got the word at 8:35a.m.: Tree 'roos! Two of them! We assumed it must be a mother and a baby. We raced after the tracker, who told us in Tok Pisin, the national trade language, that they were both in a tree "clostu"—nearby. You would think it would be impossible to get the animals out of the trees, but the trackers know exactly how. First, you build a little fence around the tree. Then one tracker climbs an adjacent tree, and the kangaroo jumps off its branch to the ground, where other trackers grab it by the strong tail and quickly stuff it into a coffee bag.

When we got the animals back to camp, we saw the "baby" was an adult male. The trackers had found two tree kangaroos on a date! For the first time in Lisa's study, she would be able to radio-collar an adult male. "This is a miracle!" she cried. "The first ever collared male Matschie's!" said her New Guinean student. "History!"

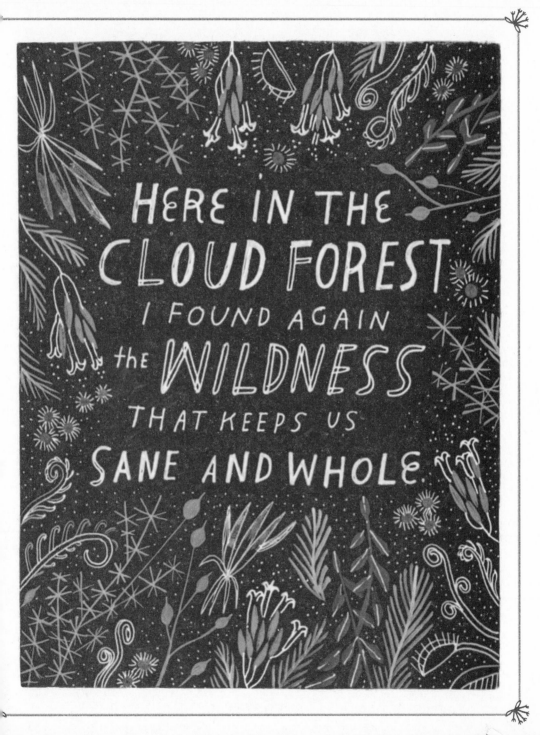

The vet lightly anesthetized the tree kangaroos to examine them and put on their radio collars without further scaring them. The female was first. She was the color of a rainforest orchid, her long tail golden, her back a deep chestnut-to-paz. Her curved claws, perfect for climbing, gleamed ocher. I couldn't help but reach out and stroke her fur, as I had once stroked Tess's. It was softer than a cloud.

As the tree 'roos, their collars on, awaited the morning's release in a large, leafy pen, we all wondered what to name them. But Lisa had already decided: Christopher and Tess.

ON THE TRAIL TO THE RELEASE SITE, MY BOOTS WEIGHED extra pounds with caked mud from the increasingly slippery trail. Their names jangled and jounced in my mind, in the rhythm of each heavy step. Tess. Chris. Tess. Chris. How many times in the fourteen years I'd shared with my pig and my dog had I uttered those sweet words? Since their death, just the sound of their names had been as an arrow to my heart. But now it was different. Tess. Chris. Tess. Chris: repeating their names became a chant, a mantra, a prayer—a call to remember my beloved ones with gratitude, and to be in the right frame of mind for this momentous release.

These beautiful wild animals were not my Chris and my Tess, of course. Nor were they inhabited by their spirits. They were their own complex, individual selves, who loved their unique lives. But also, they were, to me, wildness itself. These two animals carried within them the wild heart that beats inside all creatures—the wildness we honor in our breath and our blood, that wildness that keeps us on this spinning planet. Here in the cloud forest, I found again the wildness that keeps us sane and whole, the wild, delicious hunger for life.

The day we released Christopher and Tess back into the forest, it set me free, too.

CHAPTER 8

SALLY

*T*HE CARD SAT ON MY DESK AS A REMINDER. "LOVE IS not changed by death," read the quote by British poet Edith Sitwell, "and nothing is lost, and in the end, all is harvest."

My friends assured me that Christopher and Tess were still with me. Gretchen Vogel, who had given us our first flock of hens as a housewarming present, is a spiritual medium, and she told me she could see both Chris and Tess when she came to visit our house. The spirit of our 750-pound pig was even bigger than he was in life. He floated around after me like a blimp, she said. And she could see Tess plain as day, sitting beside me on the black and white linoleum tiles in the kitchen.

But why couldn't I see them?

I had never been a person gifted with visions or dreams or contact with spirits. In high school Bible study, to my disappointment, I never got tongues. I believe in the survival

of the soul. It is an important tenet of my faith. But to my immense frustration, I could never feel the presence of loved ones who had passed on. I only missed them. I spoke of this to a friend whom I had met in the Amazon, a martial artist and former U.S. Marine. "Oh, but you *do* feel them," he said gently. "What you are feeling when you miss them is not their absence. It's their *presence*."

His wise words soothed me. But I couldn't help but long for some sign, some feeling, some communication.

Then one night in January—after I had returned from Papua New Guinea, after I had written the memoir of my life with Christopher Hogwood, after completing the tree kangaroo book, after another research trip to the Amazon and yet another one to Italy, a year and a half after she had died—Tess came to me in a dream and showed me the promise of joy that lay ahead.

✧

I DREAM OF ANIMALS OFTEN, AND USUALLY THEY ARE RAP-turous. But this dream was different. It began with a crisis. A friend had given us a border collie puppy. What could be better? But I was beset with anxiety. In the dream, the baby was only about the size of a newborn mouse, and I was terrified it would die. I had no idea how to keep the puppy alive. I felt utterly helpless.

Then someone came to the door. I didn't hear a knock, but I knew someone was there. I opened the back door—and there stood Tess.

Oh! The joy of seeing her again! But even as I lay dreaming, I understood that Tess was dead. I knew in the dream that Tess was in her spirit form, and that she had come to help me. I raced to get Howard. He came to the door with me. But now Tess was gone. In her place stood a different border collie.

Like Tess, this border collie had a white stripe down the nose, white legs, and white tail tip. But she was even more luxuriantly furred than Tess. Her ears stood up taller, with no flop to the tips. She lacked Tess's white ruff. She looked at us expectantly with intense brown eyes.

Instantly, I understood that Tess had sent this dog to us. From the moment I woke up, I set out to find her.

✧

HOWARD AND I, UNBEKNOWNST TO EACH OTHER, HAD SEP-
arately been visiting a website for a border collie rescue. Located in rural upstate New York, it's the largest rescue devoted
to the breed in the region, if not the nation. It features appealing photos and detailed stories of dozens of border collies and
border collie mixes for adoption. Glen Highland Farm Sweet
Border Collie Rescue was the obvious place to start looking
for the dog Tess had shown me. I strongly felt she was female.
But would I recognize her?

Adopting a dog from this rescue is not easy. The dogs have
great lives on the farm. They run free over acres of fenced grass,
ponds, and woods, sleep snug and warm inside at night on dog
beds and couches, and have loads of toys, volunteers, and other
dogs to play with. No wonder the rescue only lets these dogs go to
homes that will be even better than this. To be considered as po-
tential adopters, we had to fill out a lengthy form, include photo-
graphs of our house and yard, and procure letters endorsing our
fitness for border collie stewardship from our veterinarian and
at least one neighbor. Finally, after submitting the paperwork, a
date was decided when we could visit. By this time it was Febru-
ary. We awaited a call confirming the time of our appointment.

The call didn't come in time for us to make the trip; it was a daylong drive to the farm, and we would need overnight accommodations. Disappointed, we planned for another visit several weeks later, in March. This time we'd stay overnight at Howard's parents' house in Long Island and then drive to the rescue. My heart pounded as I packed Tess's old leash, her bowls, and her blanket into the car. Howard and I had looked so many times at the different dogs profiled on the website. Which was the right one? Would she know us? Would we know her? What if I picked the wrong dog, and failed my stalwart, lionhearted Tess, who had come all the way back from the dead to try to show me the right one?

We returned from dinner the night before we were to set out from Long Island and found a message on Howard's parents' answering machine. Many of the border collies at the farm had an illness; our visit was canceled a second time.

Clearly, though many wonderful dogs awaited adoption at Glen Highland Farm, our dog was not there.

But where was she?

I CAME HOME AND LOOKED AT OTHER RESCUE SITES: Animal Rescue League of New Hampshire. Petfinder.com. Humane societies in New Hampshire, Massachusetts, Connecticut, Rhode Island, and Maine. New England Border Collie Rescue. For some reason, few border collies were available for adoption at the time, and no young females were available. I was starting to feel frantic. Now it was April, three months after Tess had come to me in the dream. It appeared not only possible, but likely, that I would fail her—and meanwhile, the dog who was meant to be ours was languishing out there, somewhere. I didn't even know where to start.

A breeder was out of the question. We knew an excellent one in the next town over, but he bred professional working dogs, not pets—and besides, we had always wanted to give a home to a border collie who wouldn't otherwise have a good one.

So, without much hope, I cast my dream upon the mercy of the universe. I told some of our friends that we were looking for a young female border collie. One friend was a *Yankee* columnist and knew, it seemed, half the population of New England. Another was on the board of the local Humane Society. A third friend had worked at the Massachusetts SPCA. Surely they would have some leads.

On a whim, I also called Evelyn—the woman who runs the private rescue where we had gotten Tess. We'd stayed friends ever since we'd brought Tess home. I had immediately told her about Tess's death, and of course, I reasoned, she would have called us if, by some fluke, she suddenly acquired another border collie—which was unlikely. Tess had been the only border collie Evelyn had gotten at the rescue in fourteen years. But I phoned her anyway, just to tell her we were looking.

Evelyn was silent for several seconds, and then replied, as if stunned:

"Well, I've got a girl right here."

✧

SHE WAS PERHAPS FIVE YEARS OLD. EVELYN WASN'T SURE. The dog had lived in two different homes before arriving at Evelyn's rescue, and neither owner appeared to care very much for her. Her name was Zooey, but she didn't come when called—Evelyn thought it sounded too much like "no-o-o"— so Evelyn had renamed her Zack.

The dog's story was pathetic. That winter, from an ill-timed coupling with the border collie next door, which Evelyn thought might have been forced, Zack had borne her owners a litter of eight valuable, purebred border collie pups. But because her people had made her breed in the winter, and then whelp on the concrete floor of the cold basement, the babies were freezing to death. Five of the eight had died before the man called Evelyn for help.

When Evelyn arrived, she found the new mother desperate, running in and out of the whelping box, aware that her pups were dying but helpless to save them. "I was sick about it," Evelyn told me. "She was practically bald and loaded with fleas. I even treated her for mange. It was all I could do not to curse those people."

Evelyn saved the three remaining pups, whom the man planned to sell for good money. But he had no use for the mother. So Evelyn took Zack and nursed her back to health. She had a full coat now, Evelyn told us. "She's a beautiful dog," she said. "But she's not very well socialized."

Howard and I went over to meet her.

✧

"Z𝐚ck! C𝐚lm down, now!" E𝐯elyn 𝐚dmonished 𝐚s the dog pulled against the leash. At first sight, Zack looked shockingly like Tess: a classic border collie, with the typical white socks, white stripe down the nose, and white ruff and chest

against a black background. But of course she was different, and soon the differences were obvious.

Zack was larger than Tess, about eight pounds heavier, furrier, with taller ears. Her temperament was utterly different. Tess had been incredibly tuned to us from the moment we met. Howard had fallen in love with Tess after his first toss of a Frisbee. But this dog, Howard noted with disappointment, ignored the flying disk. She wouldn't fetch a ball. Zack didn't seem interested in playing with toys of any kind.

She didn't respond to her old name, Zooey, *or* her new name, Zack. In fact, she didn't appear to know any English at all. Unlike with Tess, who had laser focus on us and what we were doing, everything captured Zack's attention for a moment until something new tore it away.

Howard didn't like her coat. Though it had grown back lushly after her mange treatments, and she was super furry, with some distinctive curls on her back toward her hindquarters, it wasn't ebony like Tess's but had a brown tinge to it. He didn't like her tail, which curled to the right—possibly because of some injury. He didn't like her age—five, he thought, was too old. Tess's death had broken his heart, and if we were to adopt a new dog, he wanted one we would have at least as long as we had Tess. Even though she leaned against him appealingly when they met, he didn't want her.

But I had noticed something important when I saw Zack from the side. Though she had an extravagant white ruff, it didn't go all the way around her neck. On her right side, her neck was solid black. She looked like she had no white ruff at all. This was the dog from the dream.

We visited Zack again, and still Howard couldn't bear to take her home. Beside myself, I drove off to my friend Liz Thomas's house and sobbed at her kitchen table. When I returned, Howard was in bed, the light out. In the darkness came his voice: "Let's get the dog." The next day, we drove to Evelyn's to take her home.

"Good luck!" Evelyn called as the three of us drove away. "She's a lot of dog."

✧

EVELYN WAS RIGHT. SHE WAS A LOT OF DOG. HER FIRST DAY with us, she pooped in almost every room of the house, including (though we, unfortunately, did not discover this for several days) the basement. She was also a counter surfer. No food she could reach was safe. She dug holes in the lawn, which Tess never did, and she enjoyed rolling in, as well as eating, other animals' excrement. She seemed completely innocent of any English at all.

But she was also a good learner. We renamed her Sally, which she understood from her first day with us. And after that first day, she never soiled in our house again—except for the basement, which, perhaps because she had been confined in a basement to whelp her pups, she considered an appropriate latrine.

Sally and I worked with a private trainer and took group obedience classes at two different locations. Soon her recall was perfect—she always came when called—and she would reliably obey all the other standard commands, even shaking hands on cue. At the end of a month of training, she earned her Certificate of Good Manners from the local Humane Society, which we proudly displayed on the refrigerator. But the very evening she earned it, before I served Howard his dinner, she ate his crabcakes off the plate from the kitchen counter. She ate the birthday cake I made for a friend. She opened a cabinet door in order to eat an entire box of oatmeal—with explosive results.

I liked to say "Sally does everything I ask—and so much more!" It was things we did *not* ask her to do that caused problems. Her recall was so good that she could reliably hike through the woods with us off-leash—some of my greatest daily pleasures were our morning walks alone, and our afternoon walks with my friend Jody Simpson and her standard poodles, Pearl and May. But while doing so, Sally would often eat and/or roll in something awful. Once I had to ride back from a hike hunched with Sally in the cargo hold of Jody's dark blue SUV because Sally was too smelly and sticky to ride in the back seat with the other dogs.

Another time, we were walking up a dirt road where a family of German shorthaired pointers lived. The pointers' yard had an invisible fence, keeping the resident dogs from straying. But it did nothing to prevent Sally from rushing inside the house through the dog door, disturbing a mother dog who had recently whelped puppies and somehow instigating a fight between two of the resident pointers that the owner had to break up—in so doing, acquiring a bite on her hand that required a trip to the hospital emergency room. Especially because the homeowner was a lawyer who could have easily sued, I was very grateful that she forgave Sally for causing the melee.

Sally loved to steal. She stole lunches from backpacks. She would grab a sandwich right out of your hand on its way to your mouth. One morning she seized the steel wool from the kitchen and left a trail of rusty orange splinters across the dining room rug. She opened the cabinet beneath the sink to fish items from the garbage. She always looked so proud of these accomplishments. I couldn't help but laugh. Howard called her Little Sally Rap Sheet. But when he'd drive with just the two of them in his truck, he'd sing to her the Bruce Springsteen song "Little Girl, I Want to Marry You."

Despite being the same breed, Sally and Tess were almost complete opposites. Tess was a graceful athlete. Sally knocked things over. Tess loved her Frisbee and tennis ball but disdained other toys. Sally, as it turned out, became crazy for toys—except for the Frisbee, which she would catch only grudgingly to please Howard. Tess loved us, but felt that more than a few minutes of petting was excessive, and she disliked being brushed. But Sally was extravagantly affectionate. She leaned into strangers; she pressed her snout against their faces, begging for kisses. She loved the brush and would luxuriate for over an hour while I lovingly groomed her lush fur each night. We switched her dog food and her coat lost the brown tinge Howard had disliked. Now it glowed ebony.

I felt whole again. Sally made me unspeakably happy. I loved the softness of her fur, the cornmeal-like scent of her paws, the rolling cadence of her gait, the gusto with which she ate (even the stick of butter softening for the dinner table and the bowl of cereal abandoned for a moment to take a phone call). I loved the way she'd eviscerate the stuffed toys I would always bring her from my travels—delighting in the destruction of a blue shark, a red rhino, and one stuffed hedgehog after another. I loved her tall ears. Shortly after Howard and I had graduated college, the rock group the Police came out with the hit "Every Little Thing She Does Is Magic," and that's how I felt about Sally.

The three of us slept snuggled together, all our limbs—arms, legs, tail—entwined. Unfortunately, Sally often leapt up and barked replies to distant dogs and foxes during the night. Soon after, she'd be snoring again beside us while we lay, hearts pounding, staring at the crack in the plaster ceiling for hours afterward. And if Howard got up at night, Sally would immediately and deliberately rearrange herself to take up his sleeping lane, with her head on his pillow. When he got back, she'd give him a puffy smile. She thought this was a hilarious joke. And so did we.

People often speak of a lifetime dog, a phrase that may have been coined by the author and fellow border collie owner Jon Katz. "They're dogs we love in especially powerful, sometimes inexplicable ways," he's said. Tess was our lifetime dog.

But so was Sally.

Sally was no replacement for Tess, or for Chris. She was not a serious, intense, laser-smart border collie. She was not a great big Buddha master like Christopher Hogwood. She was not a wise mentor like Molly. And yet, from the moment Sally came home, I loved her no less than I loved them.

This is the gift great souls leave us when they die. They enlarge our hearts. They leave us a greater capacity for love. Thanks to the animals before Sally, I adored her with all the love I had for Molly, all the love I felt for Tess, all the love I had for Chris—*and* all the love I had for this silly, goofy, sweet, smiley, uniquely wonderful new dog.

"Tess must be laughing at us," Howard would sometimes say as I cleaned up the bag of dog kibble Sally had strewn all over the kitchen floor, or hosed the smelly remains of a rolled-in deer carcass from her fur. I never doubted it. I loved thinking of Tess smiling down on us from heaven, knowing that every time I looked at Sally, I thought gratefully and lovingly of Tess, too. For after all, everything had turned out as Tess had intended when she came to me in the dream.

YEARS LATER, AS I WAS LOOKING OVER NOTES I HAD TAKEN from talking with Evelyn about Sally long ago, I realized another miraculous aspect to that dream. It had started with a crisis: a puppy whose life was in danger but whom I felt powerless to save. The dream had occurred in January, the same month—and, who knows? possibly the same night!—that Sally, then named Zooey, was imprisoned in a cold basement many miles away from me, desperately trying to save her freezing pups from dying. Had I glimpsed, through the dream, the heartbreaking dilemma that, without my knowing her, Sally was facing?

I wondered: Did Tess appear to Sally, too? Did she show her me, a promise of a new future? Perhaps, thanks to Tess, Sally and I had seen each other that same night, in our dreams.

CHAPTER 9
OCTAVIA

STANDING ON A SHORT STEPSTOOL, I BENT OVER THE
tank waving a dead squid back and forth in the forty-
seven-degree salt water. Finally the muscles of my hand froze.
So I switched to my left hand, until it, too, froze and I could
move it no longer. But still, despite my efforts with what I
had hoped would prove an appealing food item, the New England Aquarium's new giant Pacific octopus, a female named
Octavia, remained plastered by her suckers to the opposite
wall of her 560-gallon tank. She would not come to me—yet.
I decided to try again later. I desperately wanted this octopus
to be my friend.

Earlier that spring, I had met Octavia's predecessor, Athena. The moment the aquarist opened the heavy lid to her
tank, she slid over to inspect me. Her dominant eye swiveled
in its socket to meet mine, and four or five of her four-foot-

long boneless arms, red with excitement, reached toward me from the water. Without hesitation, I plunged my hands and arms into the tank and soon found my skin covered with dozens, then hundreds, of her strong, white, coin-size suckers. An octopus can taste with all its skin, but this sense is most exquisitely honed in the suckers.

"Weren't you afraid?" my friend Jody asked as Sally and I hiked with her and her poodles through the woods the next day. Jody and I spent hours playing with and exercising our dogs every day; like me, she is a huge animal lover. But an octopus—boneless, cold, covered with slime? "Wasn't it gross?" she asked.

"If a human had begun tasting me so early in our relationship," I admitted, "I'd have been alarmed." But this was an earthbound alien—someone who could change color and shape, who could pour her baggy forty-pound body through an opening smaller than an orange. Someone with a beak like a parrot and venom like a snake and ink like an old-fashioned pen. Yet clearly, this large, strong, smart marine invertebrate—one more different from a human than any creature I had ever met before—was as interested in me as I was in her. And that was why I was so intrigued.

I'd come back twice more to get to know Athena better. She even seemed to recognize me. Experiments I had read about, conducted at the Seattle Aquarium, proved that octopuses can and do recognize individual humans, even when the people are identically dressed and even when the octopuses are simply looking up through the water at them. Athena let me pet her head—something she'd never let a visitor do before. She turned white, the color of a relaxed octopus, beneath my touch. I had only started to know this strange and compelling creature, but already she had opened to me a possibility I'd never before explored: getting to know the mind of a marine mollusk, a creature closely related to brainless clams yet reportedly smart and sensitive.

I was working on a magazine article on octopus intelligence, which I hoped to expand to a book. Then, just one week after my third meeting with Athena, I received terrible news. Athena had died. She had likely succumbed to old age. Nobody knew for sure, as she had hatched in the wild, but Athena was probably three to five years old, the outer limit of giant Pacific octopus longevity.

I wept at the news. Only during my lifetime had scientists begun to acknowledge that chimpanzees, humankind's closest relatives, are conscious beings. But what about creatures so different from us that you'd have to go to outer space, or into science fiction, to find anything so alien? What might I discover about the interior lives of these animals if I were to use, as a tool of inquiry, not only my intellect, but also my heart? Now that Athena was gone, so, it seemed, was the opportunity for that new adventure.

But days after Athena's demise came an invitation. "There's a young pup octopus headed to Boston from the Pacific Northwest," the aquarist Scott Dowd emailed me. "Come shake hands (8) when you can."

This would prove easier said than done.

✧

"LET'S TRY AGAIN LATER. SHE MIGHT CHANGE HER MIND," Wilson Menashi, a longtime aquarium volunteer who had worked extensively with octopuses, suggested. Though Athena had seized me right away, Octavia showed no interest in meeting me—or anyone else, for that matter.

"They're all individuals," Wilson explained. "Even the lobsters have personalities." Among octopuses, personality differences are well known to those who care for them, and are often reflected in the names aquarists give them. At Seattle Aquarium, one of the octopuses was so timid that she never came out from behind the filter. They named her Emily Dickinson after the reclusive poet. Finally, because she never showed herself to the public, they released her back into Puget Sound, where she'd been initially caught. Maybe, like Emily, Octavia was just shy.

Or there could be another explanation. Usually when the octopus on public display shows signs of aging, the aquarium gets a young octopus who grows up in a large barrel behind the scenes, getting to know people, before the animal takes its place in the big octopus tank. Because Athena had died unexpectedly, the aquarium had to get a new octopus fast, and understandably wanted a big one to impress the public. Octavia wasn't as big as Athena, but her head was about the size of a cantaloupe, and her arms were about three feet long. It was clear that Octavia was not really a young pup. She was a large, perhaps nearly mature octopus who had been living wild in the ocean just weeks before.

So, even though I tried to interact with her three separate times that day, it was no wonder I got nowhere with Octavia on my first visit. It seemed I was having no better luck on my second trip. That morning, again I offered her squid to no avail. Then Scott got the idea to present the food to Octavia held in long tongs, which could be held right up to her face. Suddenly, Octavia seized the tongs—and then grabbed me. She began to pull.

Her red skin signaled her excitement. I was excited too. She had my left arm up to the elbow encased in three of hers, and my right arm held firmly in another. There was no way I could resist. A single one of her largest suckers could lift thirty pounds, and each of her eight arms had two hundred of them. An octopus's arms, by one calculation, can pull a hundred times the animal's own weight. If Octavia weighed 40 pounds, as Scott thought, that would pit my 120 pounds against her ability to pull 4,000.

But I wasn't even trying to escape. I was aware that like all octopuses Octavia could bite, hard, with her parrot-like beak inside the confluence of her arms. I knew, too, about her venom. A giant Pacific's is not, like some species, deadly, but it's toxic to nerves and dissolves flesh. An envenomated wound can take months to heal. But I felt no threat from Octavia. I felt only that she was curious. I was too.

Scott, however, didn't want to see me pulled into the octopus tank, so with Octavia tugging on one end of me, he had ahold of the other. "I thought I would end up holding your ankles!" he said once Octavia abruptly released her grip.

I hoped we had achieved a breakthrough. Now, at least, she seemed interested in me, and her interest had not seemed aggressive or dangerous. But was I reading her correctly? Reading an octopus's intentions is not like reading, for instance, a dog's. I could read Sally's feelings in a glance, even if the only part of her I could see was her tail, or one ear. But Sally was family, and in more than one sense. Dogs, like all placental mammals, share 90 percent of our genetic material. Dogs evolved with humans. Octavia and I were separated by half a billion years of evolution. We were as different as land from sea. Was it even possible for a human to understand the emotions of a creature as different from us as an octopus?

Though I had learned much from my time with Clarabelle and her eight-legged kin in French Guiana, never before had I truly become close friends with an invertebrate—much less a marine invertebrate. Even imagining that I could befriend an octopus would be dismissed among many circles as anthropomorphism—projecting human emotions onto an animal.

It's true that it's easy to project one's own feelings onto another. We do this with our fellow humans all the time. Who hasn't carefully selected a gift for a friend that failed to delight, or asked someone for a date only to be coldly refused? But emotions aren't confined to humans. A far worse mistake than misreading an animal's emotions is to assume the animal hasn't any emotions at all.

A WEEK LATER, I WAS BACK AT THE AQUARIUM. THIS TIME I had company. The producers of *Living on Earth,* the national environmental radio show, had read my magazine story and were sending the show's host, a producer, and a sound crew to record a segment on octopus intelligence. None of us—Wilson or Scott or even Bill Murphy, the head Cold Marine Gallery aquarist, who cared for Octavia every day—had any idea what Octavia would do.

As I peered into the water, Wilson selected a silvery capelin from the small bucket of fish perched on the lip of her tank. Octavia came over immediately, grabbing Wilson's hand with some of her larger suckers. I plunged my hands in and she instantly grabbed me, too. More arms curled up from the water. "Go ahead—you can touch her," Bill suggested to Steve Curwood, the host of the show. As a single sucker grasped his index finger, Steve gave a little shout. "Oh! She's grabbing ahold here!" He was enchanted.

Soon, all six of us—Bill, Wilson, Steve and I with our hands in the water, and the producer and sound recorder, watching from the edge of the tank—were overwhelmed with sensation: the sucking grasp of her tasting us, the colors playing over her electric skin, the acrobatics of her suckers and arms and eyes. We stroked her, feeling her soft, silky slime as she tasted our skin, creating red hickeys with her suction. We watched her reshape the surface of her skin, making bumps called papillae that sometimes looked like a covering of thorns and other times looked like fat goose bumps. Sometimes the papillae formed little horns over her eyes.

We decided to feed her another capelin. But when we looked at the edge of the tank, the bucket was gone.

With six humans watching, she had stolen it out from under us.

We didn't try to get the bucket back. She had let the fish fall out of it and was holding it beneath her, exploring it. But while playing with the bucket, Octavia was still also playing with us. Multitasking for an octopus is easy, because three-fifths of their neurons are not even in their brains, but in their arms. It's almost as if each arm has its own separate brain—a brain that craves, and enjoys, stimulation.

I noticed that patches of Octavia's skin had started to turn from red to white—the color of a relaxed octopus.

"She's happy!" I cried to Wilson.

"Oh, yes," he agreed. "Very happy."

THE WORLD'S SEAS ARE BLESSED WITH MORE THAN 250 SPE-cies of octopus. We know little about most of them. But the majority of the species that have been studied—the giant Pacific among them—are thought to be largely solitary. Even mating is a fraught affair, apt to turn into the kind of dinner date when one octopus eats the other. So why would an octo-pus want to be friends with a person?

The answer, I think, is to play with us.

In the wild, octopuses are constantly exploring. They eat a huge variety of foods, from clams with shells that need to

BEING FRIENDS WITH AN OCTOPUS—WHATEVER THAT FRIENDSHIP MEANT TO HER—HAS SHOWN ME THAT OUR WORLD...IS AFLAME WITH SHADES OF BRILLIANCE WE CANNOT FATHOM.

be opened, to fish that must be chased, to crabs that hide in coral crevices. But in addition to food, octopuses like to find stuff and take it home. Some species are known to collect two halves of a coconut shell and lug them quite some distance so they can pull the two halves back together around them and create their own private Quonset hut. Others bring stones back to the den and build a wall in front of the entrance. They famously steal GoPros and cameras from divers. Sometimes they'll tug on divers' face masks or regulators.

In captivity, octopuses enjoy toys, often the same ones with which children play. Octopuses like to take apart and put together Mr. Potato Head. They play with Legos. They'll unscrew the lids to jars to get a tasty crab inside—but they enjoy manipulating objects so much, they'll often screw the lid back on when they're through. To keep the many octopuses he's known occupied, Wilson, an engineer and inventor, created a series of nesting Plexiglas boxes with different locks. Octopuses enjoyed unlocking box after box to retrieve a treat inside.

Octavia enjoyed me, I think, because we liked to play with each other. Our games weren't like baseball or dolls. They were more like versions of patty cake, but with suckers. Of course, staff and volunteers at the aquarium surely loved playing with her too—but they had other duties. I was willing to play endlessly, or at least until my hands froze or her blue copper-powered blood, which affords less endurance than our iron-based blood does, ran out of energy.

Sometimes I brought her new friends to play with. I brought my friend, Liz, a pack-a-day smoker whose taste Octavia did not seem to relish. I brought another friend who studied gorillas in Africa, with whom she played happily.

A high school senior who was job-shadowing me came along another day. Octavia doused her with salt water from her funnel, right in the face!

At one point that first year with Octavia, I had to skip my weekly visit to Boston in order to attend an octopus symposium in Seattle. When I returned to the New England Aquarium and Wilson opened her tank, Octavia jetted to my side and extended her arms to me with enthusiasm as unmistakable as Sally's puffy smile. The octopus immobilized both my arms, sucking them so hard, I would have hickeys that lasted for days. We stayed together for an hour and fifteen minutes.

But it wasn't long before Octavia wanted to play no more.

✧

"Octavia is being temperamental," Bill emailed me.

Abruptly, her behavior had changed. Usually she liked to rest in the upper corner of her tank; now she sat on the bottom, or near the window facing the public, near the brightest lights. Octavia had always been a particularly colorful, often red octopus. Now she was much paler. And importantly, he told me, "She's less interested in interacting with people." These are all, he told me, signs of old age. The end of her life could be near.

I came in to see her, and she floated over to see me. But her grip was weak. Our interaction was over in fifteen minutes. I was heartbroken. Soon I'd be leaving on an expedition to Namibia for a book on cheetahs. Would she even be alive when I returned?

I returned from Namibia to find that Octavia's life, as well as my relationship with her, was profoundly different.

Her skin was as smooth as a blown-up balloon. Her face, her funnel, and her gill openings were turned to the wall. All her suckers faced inward too, holding fast to the sides of the tank and to the rock wall of her lair—all except those on one long arm that hung languidly down like a string from the balloon of her big body. Her color was pink veined with maroon except for the webbing between her arms, which was gray.

While I'd been away, Octavia had laid eggs—eventually, perhaps 100,000 of them. Pearl white, the size of rice grains, they hung in chains by the dozens, or by the hundreds. Each egg had a little black tail-like thread, which, using her dexterous suckers, she had braided together like onions. She then glued each chain to the ceiling or wall of her rocky lair. Because Octavia had not mated, her eggs were infertile. But Octavia could not know they would never hatch. The eggs were now Octavia's sole focus, just as would be the case for a mother octopus in the wild.

A mother octopus never leaves her eggs, even to eat. In the wild, that means octopuses on eggs starve themselves for the rest of their lives. At least we could offer Octavia food. On the end of long tongs, Wilson extended a fish toward our friend in her lair. Octavia sent one arm, like an emissary, over to accept it. Then, as if remembering something, a second arm followed the first, and then a third reached out to taste mine. But she released me almost instantly. "She's not friendly anymore," Wilson told me. She was busy guarding her eggs and didn't want a visit. "Let her do her job," Wilson said, closing the lid to the tank.

In those days, I mainly watched Octavia from the public viewing area. I would arrive early, before the aquarium opened, to get a clear view.

Before the crowds arrive, much of the aquarium is dark, mysterious, and intimate. Watching Octavia was like a meditation. I emptied out my mind, sweeping a space clean to let her in. To prepare to see her, I courted stillness. I let my eyes adjust, tuned my brain to switch from seeing nothing to seeing a great deal—often more than I could process at once.

Her body might be brownish, mottled with white. She might look pink. Her skin could be thorny or smooth; her eyes, coppery or silver. She might be glued to the top of her den, or plastered to its sides. But she was always, always on her eggs. One morning, her arm was under her mantle—the part that looks like a head but is really the octopus's abdomen—another arm attached by twenty-eight suckers to the ceiling of the lair. The skin between her arms hung as still as drapery. And suddenly, after twenty-five minutes of stillness, two other arms began to vigorously sweep through chains of eggs, like a person vacuuming the curtains.

At other times, she would fluff them, a different, softer motion, like you might use to plump a pillow. She also used her funnel to shoot jets of water at them, the way you might use a nozzle on a hose. Through her gill slits, she'd inhale a great breath of water, making her mantle expand like a blooming pink lady slipper orchid—and then she'd let loose with a typhoonic blast.

Egg-cleaning sometimes looked like a caress, Octavia using only the thin tips of her arms to stroke her eggs with the tenderness any mother would show to her baby. But even when she was motionless, Octavia was caring for her eggs. Much of the time, most of the eggs were hidden because she plastered her body over them, protecting them from all comers. Even though there were no predators in her tank, she would not leave her eggs.

I could not help but wish that her eggs were fertile and that her offspring would hatch. I wished that her end, which would be coming all too soon, might be vindicated, as Charlotte the spider's was, with abundant new life resulting from her careful nurturing. But eggs fertile or no, Octavia's devotion to them was profoundly beautiful. In each caress, each cleaning, each hour of steadfast protection of this mother's eggs, I could see the ancient shape of life's first love.

Thousands of billions of mothers—from the gelatinous ancestors of Octavia, to my own mother—have taught their kind to love, and to know that love is the highest and best use of a life. Love alone matters, and makes its object worthy. And love is a living thing, even if Octavia's eggs were not. Molly. Christopher. Tess . . . all were no longer living, yet I loved them no less. And, I realized, too soon, Octavia herself would be no more. But love never dies, and love always matters. And so it still fills me with gratitude that Octavia tended her eggs with such diligence and grace. For I could face the inevitable fact of her dying with the knowledge that she would do so in the act of loving, as only a mature female octopus at the end of her short, strange life can love.

IN THOSE DAYS, TO CHEER UP, I USED TO WATCH A VIDEO OF giant Pacific octopus eggs hatching. The mother, having guarded and cleaned the eggs for six months, uses her funnel to blow the tiny babies, who look like exact miniatures of herself, out of the lair and into the open ocean, where they will live as plankton until they grow heavy enough to crawl. The mother octopus uses some of her last breaths to boost her newborns out to the sea. Within days, the divers who filmed this will return to find her dead.

But six months after Octavia laid her eggs, she was still strong. Seven months passed. Eight. Some of the eggs, despite her diligent cleaning, were disintegrating and falling to the floor of her exhibit. But still she would not leave them. Nine months passed. Then ten. It seemed some sort of miracle, but Octavia remained steadfastly plastered to her eggs, still hanging on.

Then one day I came in and noticed one of her eyes was horribly swollen. There was no treating the infection; she, like her decomposing eggs, was now simply falling apart. To make her more comfortable, Bill decided to remove her from the big tank and its potentially dangerous rocks, lights, and noisy public. But would she leave her eggs?

To everyone's surprise, when Octavia tasted the touch of Bill's hand, she agreed to move into a net and from there was transferred to a quiet, dark barrel behind the scenes.

Because she had been holed up in her rocky lair, she had not looked up at our faces through the water for ten long months. I had not touched or played with her all that time. But still, after her transfer from the main display tank, I wanted to see her at least one last time.

Wilson and I unscrewed the lid to her barrel and peered in. We held a squid for her in case she wanted to eat. She floated to the top and took the squid from our hands. But she dropped it. Hunger was not what brought her to the top of the tank.

She was old. She was sick. She was weak and near death. She hadn't had any contact with us for ten months—given an octopus's life span, that's like not seeing someone for twenty-five years. But she not only remembered us, but made the effort to greet us one last time.

Octavia looked us in the eyes and gently but firmly attached her suckers to our skin. She stayed, tasting us for a full five minutes, until she sank back to the bottom.

DID OCTAVIA FINALLY REALIZE HER EGGS WERE INFERTILE? In her last days, was she comfortable? Could she know how much I cared about her? Did it matter to her?

I wish I knew, but I don't. But now, thanks to Octavia, I know something perhaps deeper and more important, perhaps best expressed by Thales of Miletus, a Greek philosopher who lived more than 2,600 years ago. "The universe," he's reported to have said, "is alive, and has fire in it, and is full of gods." Being friends with an octopus—whatever that friendship meant to her—has shown me that our world, and the worlds around and within it, is aflame with shades of brilliance we cannot fathom—and is far more vibrant, far more holy, than we could ever imagine.

CHAPTER 10
THURBER

RICK SIMPSON KNEW IT WAS ME FROM THE CALLER ID, but I didn't expect him to pick up. I'd expected to reach his wife, Jody.

"Rick?" I managed to say only his name before I started sobbing.

"Sy, are you all right? Are you hurt? Is Howard all right? Do you want me to come over?" I couldn't answer. I was hyperventilating now, and mortified. I hadn't expected to cry, and I certainly hadn't expected to do so, uncontrollably, in Rick's ear.

Jody's ear—which I'd been anticipating—would have been different. Because she, Pearl, and May had hiked with me and Sally almost every day for the past nine years, she would instantly understand my dilemma and help me sort things out.

Finally I managed to compose myself enough to tell Rick

what had happened. Nobody was hurt. Nobody was in danger. But I felt as if my life was about to turn upside down, and I didn't think I was ready.

✧

THE FIRST SIGN OF TROUBLE BEGAN ON A BEAUTIFUL, SNOWY afternoon when we were out cross-country skiing.

Sally and I were out with Jody, Pearl, and May. Sally often strayed on our walks—after all, there were enticing feces to roll in and carcasses to eat. But when I called, she'd always notice, cocking her tall ears in my direction, and after carefully considering whether my request was worth changing her plans, she'd always come back to me. But on this snowy day, as she plowed into a thicket of burrs that would take me forever to extract from her dense fur, she didn't even look up.

Sally had gone deaf.

We made accommodations. Howard and I got her a vibrating collar, and I showed her that if she looked at me when she felt its pulse, she'd get a treat. We continued our hikes in the woods with our friends. Now we avoided routes near roads, since Sally couldn't hear approaching cars. There was one benefit to her deafness. Howard and I now enjoyed nights unbroken by Sally's high-decibel conversations with foxes and distant dogs. But her hearing loss scared me. We had been together only nine years. Was Sally much older than we had thought?

I worried. Soon I was to leave on a research trip to Brazil. I'd accompany the man who had introduced me to my first octopus at New England Aquarium, Scott Dowd, on an expedition up the Río Negro, the black-water tributary that joins with the white-water Río Solimões to form the Amazon. I was working on a book for young readers about where home aquarium fish come from, and how these small, colorful fish may save the rainforest. But I hated to leave Sally. Once again, I'd be out of phone or Internet contact for weeks. If Sally's health was precarious, I would drop out of the expedition and postpone the book a year.

The week before I left, we visited our beloved vet, Chuck. Earlier that week, Sally had seemed to slip on some ice and had a slight limp. But Chuck assured me she was fine. I was good to go.

On the flight back from Brazil, I tried phoning Howard, first from Miami and then from Boston. I couldn't reach him either time. When I walked through our door, I confronted my worst fears: Sally was lying, collapsed, at the foot of the stairs, unable to stand. While I was gone, she had been stricken with what appeared to be canine peripheral vestibular disease.

✧

SALLY RALLIED, AS TESS HAD DONE BEFORE HER. WE PRAC-ticed walking inside the house. Within two weeks we could walk up and down our street. Within a month we resumed our walks with the poodles—though now our walks were shorter and flatter. Jody, Pearl, and May were patient with us. It seemed the other dogs were looking out for Sally, who was now slow and wobbly. They'd wait for her on the trail, as Tess had done for me.

Sally was enjoying life, still stealing food, still loving our hikes in the woods, still favoring us with her puffy smile. But she seemed suddenly much older. Was it arthritis? We had her x-rayed. We tried glucosamine, the same supplement that had helped Christopher. Our vet suspected it was something else.

He was right. It was a brain tumor.

✧

WE'D HAVE DONE ANYTHING TO HELP HER. WE CONSULTED with a veterinary neurologist in Maine. We were told that treatment seldom helps. We prayed that it was a slow-growing tumor. But it was not.

Over the course of a weekend, when both Howard and Jody were away, Sally lost the ability to walk, to stand, and to eat. I didn't leave her side. As long as I was touching her, she seemed calm and peaceful. Otherwise she was agitated. I carried her outside to enjoy the warm spring sunshine. My friends Liz and Gretchen came over to support us and didn't leave till Howard came home. Chuck made an emergency house call to see us. He felt it was possible she had an infection, and gave her a shot of antibiotics, hoping if she recovered we might still have some months of happiness together. But the next day, it was clear what we had to do. Chuck came to our bedroom, where Sally lay on a sheepskin. She died in my arms.

Friends phoned and visited, trying to cheer me up. Jody returned from her trip, and I walked in the leafy shade of summer with her and her dogs. My octopus book, just published, became a bestseller. But I felt no joy in the book's success, in my friends' kindness, in the beauty of New Hampshire's woods. I felt no joy at anything anymore. I felt myself spiraling into another depression. And this time, no exotic research trip was waiting to rescue me. For the first time in twenty years, it would be a full twelve months before I set out on another scheduled expedition.

And then, one morning about a month after Sally's death, Chuck called.

"We were just checking out a new litter of Dave Kennard's pups," he said.

"Bet they're cute," I replied.

I knew Dave and his talented, purebred border collies, who lived in the next town over. The dogs were famous for performing at sheep herding demonstrations all over the Northeast. Dave sold his pups for thousands of dollars, and all of them went to working farms where they would pursue careers as professional herders. Dave never sold his dogs as pets—they would be hopelessly bored in the average home—which was one reason why I hadn't called him after the dream in which Tess had shown me Sally. The other was that, with so many dogs homeless and unloved, we would never consider buying a border collie from a breeder when we were among the relative few who could provide an appropriate home for such a high-energy animal. I still felt the same way.

So why was Chuck even telling me this?

"They're cute, all right," Chuck continued. "And they're all super healthy. But there's one, a little male, with a blind eye . . ."

Working border collies depend on excellent eyesight to herd. If they can't see all the animals they're working, they can be literally blindsided by a sheep or pig or cow, and since the animals they herd are often bigger than themselves, they can be seriously injured or even killed. They use their eyes in another way, too. They can move animals with the force of their stare alone. It's called "the Strong Eye," but you really need two. It was unlikely a serious shepherd would pay thousands, no matter how smart or otherwise healthy, for this little pup.

I hung up with my heart pounding. Then I called Jody, and got Rick.

✧

I SOON SAW THAT I STILL HAD MORE LESSONS TO LEARN ON MY JOURNEY OF TRYING TO BE A GOOD CREATURE.

At lunch, Howard and I discussed all the reasons we weren't ready for a puppy. It was too soon. We were consumed with our grief for Sally. Maybe the next spring, we might consider adopting a rescue. A female. Classic black and white, with a white stripe right down the middle of the nose, like Sally and Tess. We'd want a young dog, on the small side, as Tess had been—because Sally, at forty pounds, had been difficult for me to carry up and down the stairs in the middle of the night in her old age.

We went to see the puppy anyway. Just to take a look.

We named him Thurber. The cartoonist and essayist James Thurber is one of our favorites, and he, too, had only one good eye. (The other eye was blinded by an arrow shot by his younger brother during a game of William Tell.) Since the moment we brought him home, Thurber has been the most eager, outgoing, happy creature we've ever known.

Just looking at him makes people smile. A bolt-of-lightning white stripe zigzags from the top of his head, around his good left eye, and then down the side of his black nose. He's a tricolor, with handsome brown eyebrows and one brown sock extending from his dominant left front leg down to a white foot. His enormously long tail (when he was a puppy I could carry in one hand, his tail was already fourteen inches long!) nearly touches the ground when he stands. But his tail is seldom down. Usually it's held high, like his tall ears, waving its white tip like a flag as he bounds ahead of us in the woods. Howard calls him a trail rocket. But he always turns and waits for us to catch up. He invariably comes or waits when we call. He trusts that something good is always about to happen— because it's true.

For Thurber, pretty much every moment is fun. Indoors, he loves to play with his toys, some of which, including a red ball, belonged to Tess. When he grabs and squeaks his hedgehog or his shark, one of his stuffed lambs or snakes or octopuses, or his elephant or his dragon or his duck or his hippo or his crab, we can seldom resist playing pull and chase. But if we're busy, he plays by himself, making up games in which one of his toys comes alive and he must either herd or attack it. He rolls several balls at once around the floor and chases them, sometimes herding as many as three at a time. In the woods, he selects enormous, usually forked sticks—downed saplings, sometimes longer than eight feet—and drags or carries them along the trail to impress his companions. He is so happy that he sings. He howls to the radio in the morning, particularly if it's playing something with strings or trumpets. In the car on the way to our outings, he and I howl together to his favorite CDs. He especially likes Springsteen, and one song by the indie pop group A Great Big World, appropriately titled "Say Something." Lately our favorite duet is sung to "Gracias a la Vida" (Thanks to Life). I've even composed alternative lyrics: Gracias a la vida / for giving me this dog-o / He's the very best *perro* / in the whole wide *mundo* . . .

Everyone loves Thurber, and Thurber loves everyone. He has tons of friends, both canine and human. He instantly bonded with Gretchen and Liz and Jody. We hike in the woods almost every weekday afternoon with Pearl and May. Mornings and weekends we go with one or more of his other dog friends: an athletic cattle dog named Basil, a water-loving black Lab named Shadow, and a beautiful golden retriever puppy exactly his age named August who lives on our block. Incredibly, she, too, was born with only one good eye.

We often forget Thurber has a blind eye. There's almost nothing he can't do. He flies after the ball when Howard flings it with the Chuck-It. He's fast and agile and smart, obedient and imaginative. As far as we're concerned, he is perfect and he is whole.

Every once in a while I catch sight of his blind eye in a certain light and remember he has one good eye, and one blessed eye—the blessed eye that brought him to us.

Thurber's blind eye was a genetic accident. It was also a miracle—one of several that conspired, along with our wonderful vet, to rescue me from a future that I was certain was nothing but bleak. Ever since Molly died, I had longed for a puppy, who instead of raising me I could myself raise— and in this way, I could pay forward the debt I owed my first mentor. But from trolling border collie rescue sites, I knew that border collie puppies for adoption are difficult to find. What were the chances that a pup from one of Dave's famous litters would end up with us? And the timing, which at first appeared so wrong, was freakishly perfect: Thurber arrived at the one moment of my more than thirty-year career that I had no pressing deadlines, no expeditions pending for months. I was free to devote most of the summer and fall to raising a puppy. I could give to this baby all the nurturing, confidence, and security that Tess and Sally had so tragically lacked before they had come into our lives.

Thurber was not what we were expecting. He was not even what we thought we wanted. We thought we'd wanted a dog months or years later than Thurber appeared. We had imagined a petite black-and-white female rescue with a plush double coat; we got a male tricolor with a short coat who's turning out (at less than two years old at the time of this writing) to be both the tallest and the heaviest dog in our lives. Other than being a border collie, he is unlike both Tess and Sally in so many ways. Neither Sally nor Tess particularly relished meeting new dogs; Thurber greets everyone with enthusiasm. He does things neither Sally nor Tess would do. He wakes us each morning by poking us with the white paw of his brown arm as a person might. (We've noticed his mother, whom we've gone back to visit with Thurber several times, reaches out with her arm in the same way.) Thurber doesn't like to sit in our respective offices, as did Tess and Sally, but in one of two favorite spots: in a rocking chair between my office and the kitchen, or halfway up the stairs to Howard's office, with his snout poking through the spindles of the banister and his front legs hanging down.

The most important difference, though, is that Thurber is happy no matter where he is or whom he's with. We hate to leave him, but if we need to go away for a week or a weekend and can't take him—like the recent weekend we went to Arizona for the wedding of Kate Cabot, one of the two little girls who had lived next door—Thurber can happily stay with any number of friends. That wasn't the case with Tess (if we left, we always had to leave her with Evelyn) or Sally (whom we really couldn't leave at all for more than a few hours). Though both of them were happy dogs, they both suffered from separation anxiety, having been neglected or abused when they were younger.

Thurber again surprises us with a surfeit of blessings. Not only did he heal our sorrow. He allows us to rewrite, in a way, the early sorrows of our previous dogs.

When the student is ready, the adage goes, *the teacher will appear.* This time, the student wasn't ready. The teacher came anyway. I was fifty-eight when Thurber appeared in my life, and I soon saw that I still had more lessons to learn on my journey of trying to be a good creature. Among the many truths that Thurber has taught me is this: You never know, even when life looks hopeless, what might happen next. It could be that something wonderful is right around the corner.

Sy and Molly were pups together.

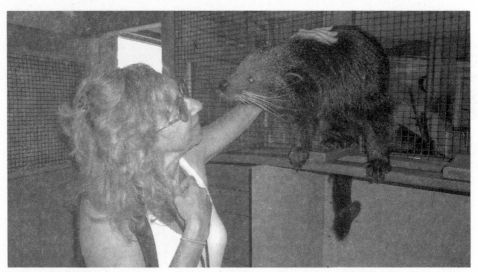

Meeting a friendly binturong at the Roger Williams Park Zoo in Rhode Island.

Sally offers her irresistible puffy smile.

Sy strokes her friend Octavia.

Enjoying the company of 18,000 snakes in the Narcisse Snake Dens, Manitoba.

In early runthood, Christopher Hogwood was small enough to fit in a shoebox . . . but with plenty of slops and love, he grew to 750 pounds.

From left to right: May, Pearl, and Sally on vacation together in Maine
(Their humans came along, too.)

By her twenties, though Sy no longer thought she was a pony, she still loved every horse
she ever met.

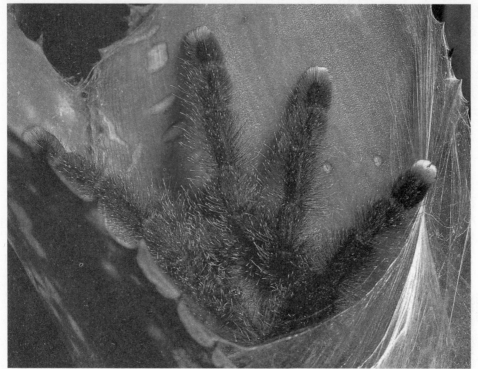

Beautiful Clarabelle rests calmly in her silken hideaway, with just a few of her pink toes peeking out.

Searching for octopuses, Sy scuba-dives with her friend and instructor Doris Morrissette in Cozumel, Mexico.

Making a new friend in Namibia—an orphaned cheetah cub turned ambassador for the Cheetah Conservation Fund.

Thurber on the trail, carrying his prize.

After her book *The Soul of An Octopus* was published, the New England Aquarium named an octopus after Sy. Here the two Sys, by then good friends, share a gentle caress, toward the end of Sy the octopus's short life.

Sally looks up while we cross-country ski.

Sy with tree kangaroo Holly at the Roger Williams Park Zoo.

As a puppy, Thurber reaches out with his brown arm.

Home sweet home: happy to live in a tent in the Outback.

Emus Bald Throat, Black Head, and Knackered Leg.

Playing with a royal Bengal tiger cub.

These black bear cubs would later be released to the wild and star in a National Geographic documentary that Sy wrote about the work of her friend, wildlife rehabilitator Ben Kilham.

This sweet cow lived at a farm in Peterborough, NH.

Despite a leg injury in her youth, Tess leaps balletically to catch her Frisbee.

Visiting with a tarantula friend at Sam Marshall's spider lab in Ohio.

Off to the Pig Plateau. Sy with slops bucket; Tess with Frisbee; Christopher Hogwood with appetite.

FOR FURTHER READING

Here are ten books that inspired me to embark on a career of studying the lives of animals and writing about the natural world.

Never Cry Wolf by Farley Mowat. One of my favorite books as a child was Farley Mowat's *The Dog Who Wouldn't Be,* which is about his adventures with his beloved pet, ignominiously named Mutt. Later I would read the author's most famous adult title, and it affected me deeply. The book is a portrait of a scientist whose findings turn him into an activist on behalf of the animals he studied. Though *Never Cry Wolf* was published as a factual account, it was later decried as fiction. Yet even as he departed from the facts on the ground, Farley's text remains true to matters of the heart. "Never let the facts get in the way of the truth," he later told me, as he generously welcomed me to his home and helped me while I researched my first book. And while I've remained a stickler for facts in my own writing, Farley showed me that a book must have emotional resonance as well if its author is to successfully move others to action.

My Life with the Chimpanzees by Jane Goodall. I grew up inspired by photos of Jane with the chimpanzees of Gombe in the pages of *National Geographic* in the 1960s, even before I could read. Finally reading the story of her life, which came out in 1988, was worth the wait.

Gorillas in the Mist by Dian Fossey. The majestic mountain gorillas in their misty cloud forest home appealed to me even more than Jane's fascinating chimps. I read Dian's memoir in its first edition, when the cover—my favorite of any book ever published—featured an intimate, close-up portrait of a silverback male, Uncle Bert, his black face benign and thoughtful, his jet fur bejeweled with raindrops. The back cover showed Uncle Bert from the other side, accentuating the great dome of his skull and the massive power of his shoulders and back.

Of Wolves and Men by Barry Lopez. One of my best friends, who later became a veterinarian, left this book on my porch as a gift before I left for the Outback. This classic, careful study of wolves' true lives and how they have been understood by human cultures through the centuries showed me the value of looking at an animal's historical and even prehistoric relationships with humans in an effort to understand its powers.

King Solomon's Ring by Konrad Lorenz. This is a classic account of animal behavior by the man who founded the field now known as ethology. His careful and detailed observations of graylag geese, crow-like jackdaws, and even cichlid fish are not only scientifically revealing, but also filled with respect and affection for each animal as an individual.

The Outermost House by Henry Beston. A quote from these pages helped me to define what I set out to do in chronicling the natural world:

> We need another and a wiser and perhaps a more mystical concept of animals. . . . For the animal shall not be measured by man. In a world older and more complete than ours, they move finished and complete, gifted with extensions of the senses we have lost or never attained, living by voices we shall never hear. They are not brethren, they are not underlings; they are other nations, caught with ourselves in the net of life and time, fellow prisoners of the splendour and travail of the earth.

The Lives of a Cell by Lewis Thomas. In these pages I found brilliant science writing by a scientist who remains dazzled by the workings of biology. Thomas, a specialist in the human immune system, musters vivid, lyrical language to convey his wonder and excitement. His theme in these twenty-nine essays is the interconnectedness of each human with all of life.

The Edge of the Sea by Rachel Carson. This title introduced me to an author whose work helped found the modern environmental movement. I bought this, her third book, as a discard at a library sale the first year I began work as a newspaper reporter. I wasn't yet an environmental reporter, but I wanted to learn about seaweeds and snails. I became a devotee of Carson's sharp eye and lyrical voice and sought out her later works, including *Silent Spring,* her sweeping exposé of the chemical poisoning of the natural world.

Lilly on Dolphins by John Lilly. The author was one of the first scientists to attempt to formally study communication with another species. Today, his book would be dismissed as too "woo-woo" to be considered science writing; the author became known as a proponent for mind-altering drugs, an enthusiasm I don't share. But when I read the book just out of college, I was deeply moved by his connection with these intelligent individuals he came to know. Though some of his ideas have been disproved, tools that were not available to Lilly at the time of his work have revealed that dolphins do possess a complex language, including personal names, known as "signature whistles," for each individual in a given pod.

Life on a Little-Known Planet by Howard Ensign Evans. The author, a Harvard entomologist, dedicated this riveting book on insect life to the book lice and silverfish that inhabited his study with him. Even though many new discoveries about insects have been reported since this book was published in 1968 (my copy, purchased as a used paperback, cost $2.45 when it was printed!), when I re-read it today, the book seems more prescient than outdated in its appreciation for the complexity of these tiny beings.

OTHER BOOKS BY SY MONTGOMERY

FOR ADULTS:

Walking with the Great Apes
Spell of the Tiger
The Curious Naturalist
The Wild Out Your Window
Journey of the Pink Dolphins
Search for the Golden Moon Bear
The Good Good Pig
Birdology
The Soul of an Octopus
Tamed and Untamed (coauthored with
Elizabeth Marshall Thomas)

FOR CHILDREN:

The Snake Scientist
The Man-Eating Tigers of Sundarbans
Encantado
Search for the Golden Moon Bear: Science and
Adventure in the Asian Tropics
The Tarantula Scientist
Quest for the Tree Kangaroo
Saving the Ghost of the Mountain
Kakapo Rescue
The Tapir Scientist
Chasing Cheetahs
Snowball the Dancing Cockatoo
The Octopus Scientists
The Great White Shark Scientist
Amazon Adventure
The Hyena Scientist

# ACKNOWLEDGMENTS

THIS BOOK BEGAN IN OUR LIVING ROOM IN HANCOCK, NEW Hampshire, while I was sitting on our couch talking with a friend.

I hadn't seen Vicki Croke in too long, and I missed her. So I was glad when, one winter day, Vicki, a busy, nationally best-selling author who also reports on animal issues for Boston's NPR news station, broke the dry spell and drove up from the city with her producer and partner, Christen Goguen, for a visit.

We walked in the New Hampshire woods with our border collie, Sally. We scanned the snow for the tracks of squirrels and deer and wild turkeys. We stroked the feathers and kissed the combs of my flock of hens, the Ladies. And though it was the original reason for the visit, by the time we sat down so Vicki could conduct her interview, it felt almost incidental.

Once back indoors, with Christen behind the camera, Vicki and I spoke of tigers, tarantulas, tapirs, and all sorts of other animals about whom I've been lucky enough to spend a career learning and writing. The interview was nearly over when Vicki asked me: "Do you feel as though you've learned, not just about an animal's natural history, but lessons about life for yourself?"

What have animals taught me about *my* life? I hadn't been asked this before. But I answered Vicki almost immediately.

"How to be a good creature."

My interview with Vicki was archived online. One day, months later, the VP and Associate Publisher of Houghton Mifflin Harcourt Books for Young Readers, Mary Wilcox, happened to watch it. She shared it with the editor with whom I often collaborate, Kate O'Sullivan. My last answer spoke to her. "This is the book you should write next," Kate told me.

You hold in your hands that book.

While this book is about the animals who taught me how to be a good creature, I owe a deep debt to humans, too. Besides Vicki and Kate and Mary, I'd like to thank some of them here.

First to thank are my mother and father. Although we had many disagreements, I always loved them. I know that in their own way, they loved me, too. I wouldn't trade my parents for any others. Without them, I would have been someone else, someone perhaps not as determined.

I thank the humans who lived the life described in this book with me. Many of these folks are named in these pages. A few who are not deserve special mention: Pearl Yusuf, Ann Wolicki, Carolyn Beyreau, Selinda Chiquoine, Gary Galbreath, and Joel Glick. Special thanks to Gretchen Vogel and Pat Winks for helping me access memories of Molly. I'm grateful to a number of folks for kindly reading and helpfully commenting on the manuscript. Among these are Jerry and Colette Price, Judith Oksner, Amy Kunze, and Rob Matz. Thank you! My thanks are also due to another person who, alas, could not read this book. But as I wrote, I imagined Anna Magill-Dohan as my ideal reader. Her intelligence, curiosity, and quirky humor continue to illuminate my view of the world.

I am additionally grateful for the help of my wonderful literary agent, Sarah Jane Freymann; for the compelling and sensitive illustrations in this book by Rebecca Green; and for the book's gorgeous design by Cara Llewellyn.

No human is more important to me than my husband, Howard Mansfield. He is the best writer I have ever known.

Yet, despite a writer's need for calm and routine, he has patiently cared for all our animals and coped with many critter emergencies during my lengthy foreign field expeditions. To his eternal credit, Howard was responsible for adopting both Christopher and Tess. And though it sometimes took some persuasion on my part, I am endlessly grateful that he welcomed Sally, Thurber, and the rest of our animal family to bless our lives.

Finally, I want to thank some more animals: my first parakeet, Jerry; ferrets Sasquatch, Scooter, Vasco da Gama, The Age of Reason, her daughter (of course) The Enlightenment, Mr. Roberts, and Nebraska; our cat, Mica; and our cockatiel, Kokopelli. Though not covered here, they deeply enriched my life and their love lives on in every page I write.

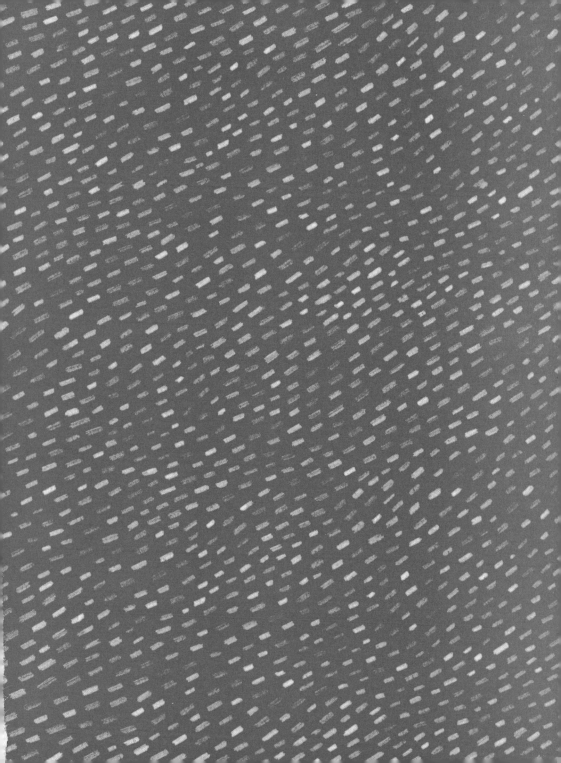

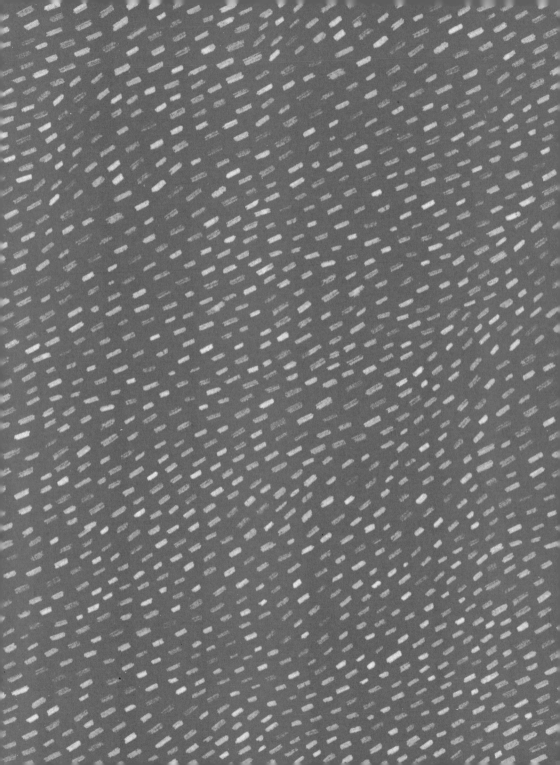